THE FOXWORTHY DOWN-HOME COOKBOOK
NO ARUGULA, NO PATÉ... NO PROBLEM!

"BIG JIM" FOXWORTHY
and JEFF FOXWORTHY

ILLUSTRATIONS BY
David Boyd

LONGSTREET PRESS
Atlanta, Georgia

Published by Longstreet Press
A subsidiary of Cox Newspapers,
A subsidiary of Cox Enterprises, Inc.
2140 Newmarket Parkway, Suite 122
Marietta, Georgia 30067

Printed in the United States of America

First printing 1997

ISBN: 1-56352-427-9

Library of Congress Card Catalog Number: 97-71938

Cover design by Jill Dible
Book design by Audrey Graham

Dedication

This cookbook is dedicated to Gloria Caddell,
who helped teach our family how to laugh, love and enjoy
good food. She was a great cook, a wonderful friend and
one of the most giving, caring people we ever knew.
We all loved her and we miss her deeply every day.

Table of Contents

Acknowledgments

Writing this cookbook was a big job that I could never have done without the help of my friends and family. Melissa, my wife, was always there to contribute, edit, enter data and test. Tracy Doan helped immensely with correcting my poor spelling and entering data. The following people helped collect recipes and get them to me: Minnie Doyle, Sandra Scott, Rose McGee, Wally Caddell, Jennifer Watts, Audrey Phillips, and Gregg Foxworthy. My thanks to all of you for making this book possible.

— JIM FOXWORTHY

THE

FOXWORTHY

DOWN-HOME COOKBOOK

NO ARUGULA, NO PATÉ... NO PROBLEM!

Introduction

A cookbook?

What does Jeff Foxworthy know about cooking? Nothing. But my daddy knows plenty. In fact, he's probably the best cook I've ever known. I say "probably" because if my wife ever challenges that statement, I have an "out" clause. She's also a terrific cook and you never want to get on the bad side of a chef. They might poison you or, even worse, stop cooking for you altogether.

Thankfully, my family is loaded with good cooks. I myself am not a chef. In fact, if you see me with a frying pan in my hand, it's probably for self-defense. I am helpful, however, at either end of the cooking process. I'm quite comfortable going to the grocery store, haggling at the Farmer's Market and even washing dishes. Some guys may scoff at that, but I'm gladly willing to clean up after someone who cooks me a good meal. Maybe I should look into doing one of those Palmolive commercials.

I'm also pretty handy at the consumption side of the equation. I come from a family of voracious eaters. It's a brave soul or a fool who reaches for the last piece of chicken at one of our family gatherings. You might well end up in the emergency room answering the question, "How did you end up with a fork in the back of your hand?"

In a long line of champions, there is perhaps none greater than my brother Jay. His appetite is the stuff legends are made of. When cows see him driving down the road, they turn and run the other way. His picture is posted on the "Beware" list at more than one all-you-can-eat buffet. To let him in the door is to flirt with bankruptcy. Once, when we were growing up, I personally saw him open a brand-new box of cereal and proceed to calmly eat the whole thing. Not bad for a five-year-old.

He is the perfect canvas on which a good cook can practice his artistry. And I do believe cooking is an art form. To watch a great chef at work is not unlike watching a painter. It is both entertaining and fascinating to witness the evolution of the thing they are creating.

I have also decided that cooking is an expression of love. It has to be to devote those long hours of preparation and work for an event that's over in a matter of minutes (not unlike sex). It must be a thrill to see others delight in something you've created. I'm sure my Uncle Roscoe felt this way before the authorities finally locked him up on counterfeiting charges.

I guess the most rewarding sight a chef can see is a table full of empty plates, bowls and platters and smiles on mouths that need the attention of napkins. "I spend all day slaving over a hot stove to cook for you, and this is the thanks I get?"

You betcha it is.

Bon Appetit and God Bless,
JEFF FOXWORTHY

COOKING AT THE FOXWORTHYS

In our clan every get-together, celebration, outing or party centered on food. Usually everyone participated in the process by bringing a favorite dish or helping in the preparation, serving or cleanup or all of the above.

We always had some hardy eaters like Jeff and his wife Gregg, Jay (Jeff's brother) and his wife Rhonda, Ronnie (Jeff's brother-in-law), William (Jeff's uncle) and his son-in-law Scott. It was a great pleasure to cook for these people because they ate a lot of whatever you cooked and made you think that they enjoyed it immensely.

In the earlier years Jay would bring some of his football teammates from Duke home with him for the weekend. These guys were fellow linemen and linebackers and were the size of elephants. They could eat everything in Georgia and still be looking for something more.

By feeding this crew, I soon came to believe that I was the best cook around, so I did more and more cooking, gained more and more confidence, and over time became a pretty fair country cook.

Cooking, eating and loving are the favorite activities of this clan and that's probably why they are so good at doing all three.

JIM FOXWORTHY

SOUTHERN COOKING

Fried Chicken

Fried chicken has been the Sunday dinner of Southerners for generations. It was what you served when you had really special company. It was what you took to church when they had a revival with dinner on the grounds.

Although all Southerners and many others cook fried chicken, few are able to get consistently that special flavor and the right amount of crunchy crust. The secret to really good fried chicken is keeping it simple.

This begins by soaking the chicken overnight or at least for 4 hours in salty water or buttermilk. Either one will give it a great flavor and make it tender. (Try both.)

2 quarts salty water or buttermilk to cover chicken completely
(add 2 tablespoons salt to water)
1 chicken, cut into serving pieces
1 cup flour
2 teaspoons salt
1 teaspoon black pepper
1 quart oil (or enough for 1 inch in fryer).

GRAVY:
1/2 cup oil used to fry chicken
3 tablespoons flour
1 cup milk

■ Remove chicken from liquid and pat dry with paper towels. (Note: The wetter you leave the chicken, the thicker the coating you will have.) Place large pieces of chicken one at a time in a plastic bag filled with 1 cup flour, salt and black pepper. Shake until coated. (Smaller pieces can be coated two at a time.) Refrigerate for 1 hour or longer.

■ Fill large, heavy pan (a well-seasoned cast-iron skillet is ideal) with 1 inch of oil and heat to medium-high heat. Add chicken but do not crowd. Cook uncovered for 7 minutes or until well-browned, turn the chicken and cook for another 5 minutes or until browned on other side. Reduce heat to medium-low, cover and cook 30 to 40 minutes. Uncover and cook on medium-high 10 minutes to crisp. Remove chicken from pan and drain on paper towels. Reserve 1/2 cup of oil for pan gravy. Serve warm.

■ To make gravy, heat oil to medium-high. Add 3 tablespoons flour and mix to form a paste. Cook, stirring constantly, until flour begins to brown. Reduce heat to low and add milk. Stir constantly until mixture begins to bubble, adding milk if needed for the desired consistency. Serve hot with chicken. Rice is a natural complement to fried chicken with pan gravy. Homemade Country Biscuits and Turnip Greens complete the meal in excellent Southern style.

⊙━━━◯ SERVES 4.

Note: *Later you may want to try slight variations to the coating. For different flavoring, add paprika and/or powdered garlic to the coating mixture. If you want to experiment with different amounts of coating, start with a fairly dry chicken and move to a thicker coating by leaving more moisture on the chicken. Using a large skillet or frying pan is important and it's key that the pieces of chicken are not crowded. Be sure to let the oil get hot before adding chicken and cook half the chicken at a time.*

Meat Loaf

The best vegetable to serve with meat loaf is ketchup! —JEFF

MEAT LOAF:
1 pound ground beef
1 pound ground pork
2 eggs
1 cup bread crumbs (plain or seasoned)
1 medium onion, chopped
2 tablespoons prepared mustard
1/2 cup ketchup
1/2 teaspoon salt
1/2 teaspoon pepper
2 shakes Tabasco

TOMATO SAUCE:
1 tablespoon butter
1 tablespoon flour
4 tablespoons ketchup
1 tablespoon vinegar
1 teaspoon sugar
1/2 cup beef broth
1 tablespoon Worcestershire sauce
2 shakes salt
2 shakes pepper
2 shakes Tabasco

MEAT LOAF:

■ Preheat oven to 350 degrees. Spray loaf pan with nonstick cooking spray. Mix all meat loaf ingredients; mold into loaf pan. Bake 45 minutes to 1 hour. Cover top with tomato sauce, slice and serve.

TOMATO SAUCE:

■ Heat butter and flour until flour begins to brown. Add other ingredients. Heat and stir for 10 minutes. Serve over meat loaf with some on the side. Great with Mashed Potatoes or Potato Casserole.

SERVES 4.

BECAUSE WE WERE SUCH FINICKY EATERS AS KIDS MY MOTHER USED TO SNEAK VEGETABLES INTO US VIA MEAT LOAF. ONCE, SHE GRATED CARROTS UP REALLY SMALL AND MIXED THEM WITH THE MEAT. ANOTHER TIME SHE TRIED TO SNEAK IN A CAN OF SPINACH. OF COURSE, THAT DIDN'T WORK BECAUSE AFTER ABOUT 30 MINUTES IN THE OVEN THE CAN EXPLODED. THERE WAS MEAT LOAF EVERYWHERE!

Pot Roast

*N*ot to be confused with the
popular hippie recipe of the 1960s. —Jeff

Note: *Marinating time is 2 to 4 hours. Cooking time is 3 hours.*

1 5-pound beef roast (chuck or rump roast)
Meat tenderizer
Garlic powder
Black pepper
Worcestershire sauce
2 tablespoons peanut oil
2 cans beef broth
6 large potatoes, cut into 1-inch cubes
2 pounds carrots
5 stalks celery
3 large Vidalia or Texas sweet onions
1 pound sliced mushrooms
2 cups cut up broccoli
2 teaspoons salt
2 teaspoons pepper
1 teaspoon garlic powder or 2 garlic cloves, finely chopped

GRAVY:
1 cup roast juices
2 tablespoons flour

■ Marinate roast by sprinkling generously with meat tenderizer, garlic powder and black pepper, sprinkle with Worcestershire and rub into meat. Refrigerate 2-4 hours.

■ Preheat oven to 325 degrees. Heat a large heavy frying pan to high heat, add oil and brown roast on all sides. Save drippings. Move roast to large roasting pan and add beef broth, vegetables and seasonings. Cover and cook in oven for 3 hours.

■ To make the gravy, pour juices from roasting pan into a frying pan over high heat and stir constantly until reduced by half. Add flour and stir constantly until gravy thickens. Serve with roast and vegetables.

SERVES 6.

Stuffed Pork Chops

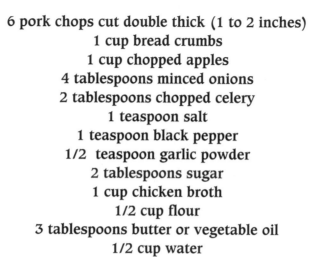

6 pork chops cut double thick (1 to 2 inches)
1 cup bread crumbs
1 cup chopped apples
4 tablespoons minced onions
2 tablespoons chopped celery
1 teaspoon salt
1 teaspoon black pepper
1/2 teaspoon garlic powder
2 tablespoons sugar
1 cup chicken broth
1/2 cup flour
3 tablespoons butter or vegetable oil
1/2 cup water

■ Cut a pocket in each pork chop. Mix next eight ingredients, stir well and moisten with chicken broth. Fill each pocket with mixture and fasten pockets with toothpicks. Dredge chops in flour and cook in oil in heavy skillet until lightly browned. Add water, cover and cook slowly over low heat for 1 1/2 hours or until tender. Add water as needed while cooking. Turn chops at least once during cooking. Remove to absorbent paper and serve warm.

SERVES 6.

Fried Fish

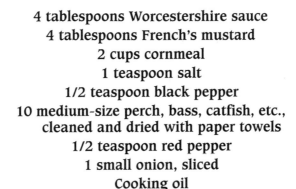

4 tablespoons Worcestershire sauce
4 tablespoons French's mustard
2 cups cornmeal
1 teaspoon salt
1/2 teaspoon black pepper
10 medium-size perch, bass, catfish, etc.,
cleaned and dried with paper towels
1/2 teaspoon red pepper
1 small onion, sliced
Cooking oil
lemon, cut into wedges

■ Combine Worcestershire and mustard into a thin paste and set aside. Combine cornmeal, salt and black pepper in a 1-gallon freezer bag, mix well and set aside.

■ Season fish inside and out with salt and pepper. Dip fish in mustard mixture and then shake fish, one at a time, in cornmeal mixture. Place a slice of onion in the cavity of each fish and let sit for 10 minutes.

■ Place 2 inches of oil in skillet and heat (hot but not smoking). Place fish in oil. Do not let fish touch; do not crowd. Brown on both sides, being careful not to over cook. Remove to serving platter and drain on paper towels. Serve hot with lemon wedges.

SERVES 6.

Note: *Onion will eliminate fish odor but will not affect taste.*

Country Ham

3 large slices country ham
2 tablespoons cooking oil

RED-EYE GRAVY:
1 tablespoon flour
1/2 cup strong coffee

■ Soak ham overnight (or at least 3 hours) in cold water, drain and dry on paper towels.

■ Cook ham in oil over medium heat for 15 minutes, turning often, and remove to warm platter.

■ To make red-eye gravy, add flour to pan and stir until it forms a paste. Add coffee and stir vigorously until smooth. Serve over ham or grits.

SERVES 4.

VARIATION ON RED-EYE GRAVY:
LEAVE OUT FLOUR AND INCREASE COFFEE TO 1 CUP. COOK UNTIL REDUCED BY HALF, STIRRING REGULARLY.

Chicken and Rice

1 fryer (3 to 4 pounds)
1 medium onion, chopped
1 cup celery, cut into 1/4-inch lengths
1 green pepper, chopped
1 cup sliced mushrooms
4 tablespoons butter
1 teaspoon salt
1 teaspoon black pepper
1/2 teaspoon garlic powder
1 can green peas, or 1 cup frozen green peas
2 cups long grain rice

■ Place fryer in stockpot. Cover with salted water and boil until done. Remove, debone and cut into small pieces. Continue to boil broth until reduced by half.

■ Sauté onions, celery, pepper and mushrooms in butter and add to stock. Add remaining ingredients and simmer for 30 minutes on low heat, adding stock or water as needed. Add chicken and cook for 20 more minutes on low heat.

SERVES 6.

Country Fried Steak

*T*he *meal every doctor recommends.* —Jeff

3 pounds sirloin or round steak, cut into 6-ounce portions
Meat tenderizer
Garlic powder
Black pepper
Worcestershire sauce
1 cup flour
1 teaspoon salt
1 teaspoon black pepper
1 teaspoon garlic powder
1 stick butter or margarine
1/2 cup vegetable oil
2 cups milk

■ Sprinkle all sides of steaks with meat tenderizer, garlic powder, black pepper and Worcestershire and rub into meat. Cover and refrigerate for a minimum of 4 hours.

■ Mix flour and salt, pepper and garlic powder well and place in a large (gallon-size) plastic bag. Add steaks one at a time and coat completely with mixture.

■ Brown both sides of steak in butter over medium-high heat. Remove steaks and add 1/2 cup of batter mix and oil to skillet and heat, stirring until mixture begins to brown. Lower heat to simmer, add milk and stir. Return steak to skillet, cover and simmer for 30 minutes.

Serves 6.

Brunswick Stew

1 hen (4 to 5 pounds)
1 pound pork tenderloin
1 pound ground beef
1 can whole kernel corn
1 can okra
2 cans tomato sauce
1/2 bottle ketchup
1 large onion chopped
1 teaspoon oregano
1 teaspoon salt
1 teaspoon red pepper
1 teaspoon black pepper
1 teaspoon Worcestershire sauce
1/2 teaspoon Tabasco sauce (or more to taste)
2 teaspoons vinegar
2 teaspoons red cooking wine
Chicken broth or Mr. & Mrs. T's Bloody Mary Mix (optional)

■ Cut up hen and parboil with pork in water. In a large stew pot, combine and cook remaining ingredients at low temperature. Grind deboned chicken and pork and add to other ingredients. Simmer for 2 hours, seasoning to taste. Add chicken broth or Mr. & Mrs. T Bloody Mary Mix if needed for thinning the stew.

SERVES 8.

Beef Stew

3 pounds stewing meat or round steak,
trimmed of all fat and cut into bite-size pieces
2 tablespoons cooking oil
2 cans beef broth/bouillon
1 large onion, chopped
4 large potatoes, cut into 1-inch cubes
3 carrots, cut into 1/4-inch slices
1 green pepper, chopped
1 pound fresh mushrooms, chopped
3 stalks celery, cut into 1/4-inch slices
2 cans crushed tomatoes with juice
1 cup okra, cut into 1/2-inch slices

■   Brown meat in oil and place in stockpot. Add all other ingredients and simmer 2 to 3 hours, adding broth as needed. Serve with corn bread and salad.

SERVES 8.

Black-Eyed Peas

1 large onion, chopped into 1/4-inch cubes
1 1-pound bag dried black-eyed peas
2 cans chicken broth
2 pieces ham hock
1 teaspoon salt
1 teaspoon pepper
1 teaspoon garlic powder or 1 clove fresh garlic, minced

■ Add onion to Crock-Pot. Wash peas and pour over onions. Cover with broth by about 1 inch (add water if needed). Add remaining ingredients and cook on high heat for about 4 hours, adding water as needed. Lower to medium heat and continue to cook until ready to serve.

SERVES 6.

VARIATIONS:
1. ADD A POUND OF HOT ITALIAN SAUSAGE. CUT SAUSAGE INTO 1-INCH LENGTHS AND SAUTÉ UNTIL BROWN THEN ADD TO PEAS.
2. ADD 1 CAN CRUSHED TOMATOES TO EITHER OF THE ABOVE.

STOVE-TOP METHOD:
■ Soak peas overnight. Sauté onions in a spoon of bacon grease, butter or the grease from the Italian sausage. Add ingredients in the same sequence as before and cook on medium-high heat for 1 hour or until tender.

PRESSURE-COOKER METHOD (SOAKING NOT REQUIRED):
■ Place all ingredients in pressure cooker and cook for 12 minutes. This is a great way to cook black-eyed peas. It's quick and the flavor is excellent.

Hoppin' John

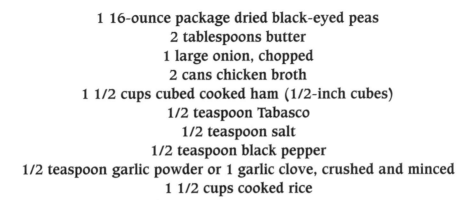

1 16-ounce package dried black-eyed peas
2 tablespoons butter
1 large onion, chopped
2 cans chicken broth
1 1/2 cups cubed cooked ham (1/2-inch cubes)
1/2 teaspoon Tabasco
1/2 teaspoon salt
1/2 teaspoon black pepper
1/2 teaspoon garlic powder or 1 garlic clove, crushed and minced
1 1/2 cups cooked rice

■ Wash black-eyed peas and soak overnight in salty water.

■ In a large pot, sauté onions in butter, add chicken broth, black-eyed peas, ham cubes and seasonings and cook on medium-high heat for 20 minutes. Lower to medium-low heat and cook for 2 hours, adding water as needed. Add rice and cook 30 more minutes. With a little corn bread this is a meal in itself.

SERVES 6.

Fried Corn

*You might be a redneck if you
think candy corn is a vegetable.* —JEFF

12 ears fresh corn
4 strips bacon
1 tablespoon sugar
3/4 teaspoon salt
1/2 teaspoon black pepper
1 cup heavy cream

■ Cut corn from cob with sharp knife and scrape milk from cob. Set aside.

■ Cook bacon in iron frying pan; remove when crisp, mince and set aside. Cook corn in bacon grease over medium heat for 10 minutes. Stir often or it will stick easily. Add seasonings and continue to stir regularly. When seasonings are well blended, add bacon. Cook for 30 minutes stirring regularly, add cream and cook on low for 10 minutes. Serve hot. It's the best!

SERVES 6.

Stewed Tomatoes

4 ripe fresh tomatoes, peeled and diced
1 small onion, diced
1 1/2 teaspoons sugar
1 teaspoon salt
1/2 black pepper
1/2 teaspoon garlic powder
1 tablespoon butter, melted
1 tablespoon flour

■   Place tomatoes in 2-quart saucepan and cover with water. Add onion and seasonings and boil rapidly until vegetables are soft. Add melted butter mixed with flour and cook 10 more minutes, stirring constantly. Great served with black-eyed peas!

⬤━━◯ SERVES 4

Fried Okra

2 pounds okra
1 cup cornmeal
1 cup flour
1 teaspoon salt
1 1/2 quarts cooking oil

■   Wash okra thoroughly in cold water and slice into 1/2-inch pieces —
discard stems and tips. While okra is wet, place in plastic bag with cornmeal, flour and salt. Shake well, making sure okra is thoroughly coated.
Fry in hot oil until golden brown. Remove and place on paper towel to
drain. Serve hot!

SERVES 6.

Fried Green Tomatoes

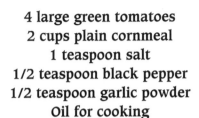

4 large green tomatoes
2 cups plain cornmeal
1 teaspoon salt
1/2 teaspoon black pepper
1/2 teaspoon garlic powder
Oil for cooking

■ Slice tomatoes into 1/4-inch slices. Put cornmeal, salt, pepper and garlic powder in a plate or pan and mix well. Dredge tomatoes on both sides and let rest on wax paper. Do not stack. Fill frying pan with 1/4 inch oil and heat to medium-high. Fry tomato slices until lightly brown. Do not crowd. Remove and drain on paper towels. Keep warm until served.

Serves 4.

Potato Salad

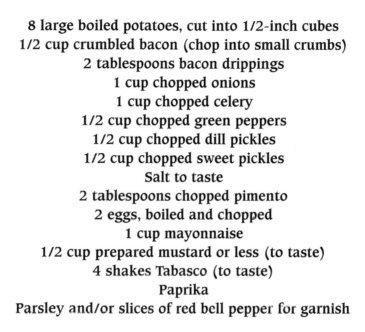

8 large boiled potatoes, cut into 1/2-inch cubes
1/2 cup crumbled bacon (chop into small crumbs)
2 tablespoons bacon drippings
1 cup chopped onions
1 cup chopped celery
1/2 cup chopped green peppers
1/2 cup chopped dill pickles
1/2 cup chopped sweet pickles
Salt to taste
2 tablespoons chopped pimento
2 eggs, boiled and chopped
1 cup mayonnaise
1/2 cup prepared mustard or less (to taste)
4 shakes Tabasco (to taste)
Paprika
Parsley and/or slices of red bell pepper for garnish

■ Place potatoes in a large bowl and stir in each remaining ingredient as listed, mashing potatoes somewhat in the process. Sprinkle with paprika and garnish with parsley and/or slices of red bell pepper. Chill.

SERVES 8.

Turnip Greens

2 pounds fresh turnip greens (2 to 3 bunches)
6 tablespoons browned butter
2 teaspoons coriander
2 teaspoons bacon drippings
1/2 teaspoon salt
1/2 teaspoon pepper
1 teaspoon sugar
2 cans chicken broth

■   Place all ingredients in large covered pot. Bring to a boil, then reduce heat and cook gently until tender, about 30 minutes. Serve with corn bread for soppin' the pot likker.

SERVES 6.

Potato Soup

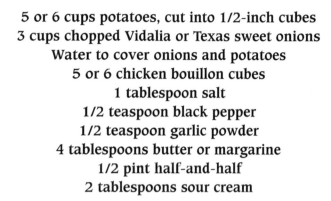

5 or 6 cups potatoes, cut into 1/2-inch cubes
3 cups chopped Vidalia or Texas sweet onions
Water to cover onions and potatoes
5 or 6 chicken bouillon cubes
1 tablespoon salt
1/2 teaspoon black pepper
1/2 teaspoon garlic powder
4 tablespoons butter or margarine
1/2 pint half-and-half
2 tablespoons sour cream

■   Bring potatoes and onions to a boil in salty water. Add bouillon cubes and simmer for 30 to 45 minutes. Remove half of the potatoes and onions and put through a blender or a mixer. Return to pot and add seasonings, butter, half-and-half and sour cream. Heat but do not boil. Serve with crackers and cheddar slices for a hearty meal.

VARIATIONS:
YOU MAY USE 2 CANS OF CHICKEN BROTH AND ADD WATER TO COVER INSTEAD OF BOUILLON CUBES. ANOTHER GOOD VARIATION IS TO ADD 1 CAN OF CREAM OF CHICKEN SOUP.

SERVES 6.

Sweet Potato Casserole

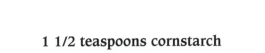

1 1/2 teaspoons cornstarch
1/4 teaspoon salt
6 tablespoons butter
3/4 cup brown sugar
1 1/2 cups orange juice
2 23-ounce cans sweet potatoes, drained

TOPPING:
3/4 cup brown sugar
6 tablespoons melted butter
1/4 cup chopped pecans
1/4 cup all-purpose flour

■ Preheat oven to 350 degrees. Combine cornstarch, salt, butter, sugar and orange juice. Cook stirring constantly until thickened. Mash potatoes and mix with sauce. Place in a casserole dish, cover with topping and cook for 1 hour.

■ To make topping, combine ingredients. Mixture will be crumbly.

SERVES 6.

Recipe courtesy of
Rose McGee,
Hilton Head, South Carolina

Mashed Potatoes

6 large potatoes, peeled and cut into 1/2-inch cubes
1/2 cup heavy cream
3 tablespoons sour cream
1 teaspoon salt
4 tablespoons butter

■ Cover potatoes with water in large pot and boil for 25 minutes or until tender. Drain and mash with a potato masher until fairly smooth. Return to medium-low heat and add cream, sour cream, salt and butter. Stir thoroughly.

⊃ SERVES 6.

Baked Potatoes

IN MICROWAVE:

■ Puncture potatoes with a fork on all sides. Cook for 5 minutes per potato. Turn and cook for equal time on the other side. Test with fork. Turn and cook 2 more minutes if needed. Remove, wrap in foil and keep in warm oven until served.

IN OVEN:

■ Cook potatoes, wrapped in foil, at 450 degrees for 1 hour, turning them one-quarter every 15 minutes. (The use of potato nails through each potato will reduce cooking time by one-third.)

Note: *If you have more than six potatoes, it is just as quick to use a conventional oven.*

Twice Baked Potatoes

2 sticks butter
1 cup chopped onions
6 medium potatoes, baked
1/2 cup sour cream
1/2 cup heavy cream
2 teaspoons salt
1/2 teaspoon pepper
2 tablespoons chives
1 cup grated sharp cheddar cheese

■   Preheat oven to 350 degrees. Melt butter in skillet and sauté onions until clear and tender. Cut potatoes in half lengthwise and scoop out pulp, being careful not to break through the skins. Mash potato pulp in bowl and add sautéed onions, sour cream, heavy cream, salt, pepper and chives. Mix well to a creamy consistency. Refill potato skins with mixture, sprinkle with grated cheese. Return to oven at 350 degrees for 15 minutes.

Serves 8-10.

Note: *This is a great "cook ahead" dish. Potatoes can be refrigerated or frozen prior to the final cooking.*

Coleslaw

1 medium head cabbage, finely shredded
1 carrot, shredded
1 onion, grated
1/2 cup mayonnaise
1 teaspoon lemon juice
2 teaspoons vinegar
1 teaspoon sugar
1 teaspoon salt
1 teaspoon pepper
1 teaspoon prepared horseradish

■　Mix vegetables together in large salad bowl. Add remaining ingredients and mix well.

VARIATIONS:
ADD 1/2 CUP SHREDDED GREEN PEPPERS AND/OR ADD 3 TABLESPOONS GRATED APPLE.

SERVES 8.

Potato Casserole

4 large Irish potatoes
2 large Vidalia or Texas sweet onions
1 stick butter
Salt
Pepper
1 cup sour cream
4 green onions, chopped

◾ Preheat oven to 375 degrees. Cut potatoes, onions and butter into 1/4-inch slices. Place 4 slices of butter in the bottom of a 2-quart casserole. Alternate layers of overlapping potatoes with layers of onions and butter. Sprinkle each layer with salt and pepper. Continue until all slices are used. Spread the top with sour cream and sprinkle with green onions. Bake for 1 hour.

VARIATIONS:
1. SUBSTITUTE CHIVES FOR GREEN ONIONS.
2. COOK ABOUT 40 MINUTES, THEN SPRINKLE A CUP OF SHREDDED SHARP CHEDDAR CHEESE ON TOP AND COOK FOR THE REMAINING 20 MINUTES.
3. SPRINKLE CRUMBLED BACON ON TOP WITH THE GREEN ONIONS AND CHEDDAR CHEESE.

SERVES 6-8.

Rice

Rice is a simple dish to prepare but many people struggle with getting it nice and fluffy. One simple method follows.

1 cup chicken broth
1 cup water
1 teaspoon salt
1 teaspoon cooking oil
1 cup rice

■ Add chicken broth, water, salt and cooking oil to a 2-quart saucepan and bring to a boil. Slowly add rice. Cook uncovered on medium heat until the water can no longer be seen in the "holes." Cover, reduce heat to low and cook 20 minutes. Toss rice with a tablespoon of butter and serve. Your rice will be perfect.

SERVES 4.

Tips: *Never stir rice while it is cooking.*
Once covered, do not uncover rice until it is done.
If you want sticky rice, cover sooner (while water is still seen in the "holes").

Country Gravy

COUNTRY GRAVY:
- Add equal amounts of flour and oil (4 tablespoons) and stir until flour begins to brown. Lower heat and add 2 cups whole milk. Stir vigorously until the desired consistency is reached. Add salt and pepper to taste. Add milk if needed for right consistency.

CHICKEN GRAVY:
- After frying a chicken, scrape pan and pour scrapings and juices into measuring cup. Skim off the grease. Pour 4 tablespoons of the remainder into small skillet and add equal amount of flour. Cook and stir slowly until flour begins to brown. Add 2 cups milk, stir and cook slowly until it reaches desired consistency. Serve immediately.

ROAST GRAVY:
- Collect juices and scrapings from roasting pan and remove fat. Add to saucepan equal amounts of drippings and flour. Stir until golden brown. Add beef broth (1 cup for every 2 tablespoons flour), stir vigorously and add milk to maintain the proper consistency. If a dark color is desired, add more broth or water instead of milk.

Country Biscuits

2 cups all-purpose flour
3 teaspoons baking powder
1 teaspoon salt
1/2 cup vegetable oil
1 cup whole milk or buttermilk

■ Preheat oven to 450 degrees. Mix dry ingredients. Add oil and cut in until coarse crumbs form. Add milk and stir until mixture is moist. Place on floured board, knead just enough to make dough hold together (too much handling makes the biscuits tough), roll out to 1/2-inch thickness, cut with biscuit cutter and place biscuits on a greased baking sheet. Bake for 20 minutes or until brown. Serve with butter and jam or preserves.

SERVES 6.

YOU OFTEN SEE RECIPES THAT BEGIN WITH THE WORD "COUNTRY," BUT NONE THAT BEGINS WITH THE WORD "CITY." WHY? MY GUESS IS THAT COUNTRY JUST SOUNDS MORE APPETIZING. THERE'S COUNTRY GRAVY, COUNTRY BISCUITS, COUNTRY-STYLE GREEN BEANS. MY DAD EVEN HAS A RECIPE FOR COUNTRY-FRIED DOVE. AS OPPOSED, I GUESS, TO CITY-FRIED DOVE, WHICH IS PROBABLY JUST A PIGEON THAT'S BEEN HIT BY A BUS.

Hush Puppies

*M*y brother's friend Scooter once listed hush puppies as his favorite seafood. We continue to pray for him. —JEFF

1 1/2 cups plain cornmeal
1/2 cup all-purpose flour
1 teaspoon baking powder
1/2 teaspoon baking soda
1 teaspoon salt
1 small onion, diced
1 egg, lightly beaten
1 teaspoon honey
Buttermilk
Cooking oil

■   Mix all ingredients except buttermilk. Gradually add buttermilk and stir to the consistency desired. (Mixture should be thick.) Drop by the tablespoon into hot oil and cook until golden brown. Hush puppies will turn themselves when done and brown on other side.

VARIATION:
ADD 1 OR 2 MINCED JALAPEÑO PEPPERS TO MIXTURE. HOT AND GOOD!

SERVES 6.

Hush puppies are a must with fried fish!

Corn Bread

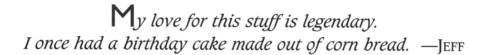

*My love for this stuff is legendary.
I once had a birthday cake made out of corn bread.* —JEFF

1 cup cornmeal
1 cup all-purpose flour
1 teaspoon salt
2 tablespoons sugar
2 teaspoons baking powder
1/4 cup cooking oil
1 cup milk or buttermilk

■ Preheat oven to 425 degrees. Mix dry ingredients well. Add oil then milk and stir well. Heat well-seasoned iron skillet, wipe with oil and pour in ingredients. Bake for 45 minutes or until golden brown. Remove and let cool for a few minutes and place on serving plate. Serve warm with butter.

Corn Pone

This is great with Brunswick Stew!

1 cup cornmeal
1 teaspoon salt
3/4 cup boiling water
1 tablespoon bacon drippings

■ Combine cornmeal and salt and mix thoroughly. Add boiling water and stir to make a thick batter.

■ Heat bacon drippings in heavy skillet over medium-high heat and pour into mixture. Stir and pour batter into skillet. Brown on both sides, remove and serve hot with butter.

SERVES 6.

Tomato Gravy

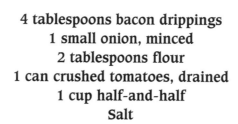

4 tablespoons bacon drippings
1 small onion, minced
2 tablespoons flour
1 can crushed tomatoes, drained
1 cup half-and-half
Salt
Pepper

■ Sauté onions in bacon drippings until onions are clear and tender. Add flour, tomatoes and half-and-half and heat (do not boil). Stir until gravy thickens, add salt and pepper, stir and serve. Good served over rice, grits, black-eyed peas and some casseroles.

SERVES 6.

Note: *This recipe originated during the Depression and was used as a main dish by many during hard times.*

CAJUN COOKING

Special Gumbo

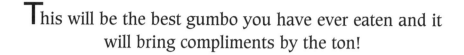

This will be the best gumbo you have ever eaten and it will bring compliments by the ton!

1 chicken
2 cups chocolate Brown Roux (see page 44)
3 large onions, chopped
2 green peppers, coarsely chopped
3 cups celery, cut into 1/4-inch slices
1 pound sliced mushrooms
2 cups okra, cut into 1/2-inch slices
1 cup chopped green onions
2 cloves garlic, crushed and minced
2 teaspoons salt
1 teaspoon black pepper
1 teaspoon Tabasco
1 16-ounce can crushed tomatoes
3 bay leaves
1/2 teaspoon thyme
3 tablespoons ketchup
3 tablespoons Worcestershire sauce
1 pound cooked ham, cut into 1/2-inch cubes
2 pounds shrimp, shelled and deveined
1 can oysters cut into small pieces
1 pound catfish fillets, cut into 1/2-inch cubes
1 pound sea scallops

■ Cover chicken with water and boil until very tender. Remove chicken, debone and cut into bite-size pieces. Reserve broth and reduce by half. Add vegetables and garlic to hot roux and sauté for 15 minutes in a large heavy skillet. Transfer vegetables and all remaining ingredients except for seafood to chicken broth. Simmer for 1 1/2 hours. If additional liquid is needed add chicken broth or Mr. & Mrs. T's Bloody Mary Mix.

■ Add seafood and simmer for 20 more minutes. Serve over rice in large gumbo bowls.

SERVES 8.

Note: *Gumbo freezes well and will be even better the second time.*

MY WIFE GREGG IS FROM LOUISIANA, SO I'VE LEARNED A LITTLE ABOUT CAJUN COOKING. MOSTLY I'VE LEARNED THAT IF IT CRAWLS, SWIMS, OR FLIES, THEY WILL EAT IT. I'VE ACTUALLY SEEN HER RELATIVES IN THE KITCHEN HITTING A BOILING POT WITH A WOODEN SPOON YELLING, "GET BACK IN THERE!"

I'VE ALSO LEARNED THAT WHEN DINING WITH PEOPLE WHO VIEW THE SWAMP AS A GIANT BUFFET, IT'S OFTEN IN YOUR BEST INTEREST NOT TO ASK TOO MANY QUESTIONS. MANY TIMES I HAVE SAID, "MAN, THIS IS DELICIOUS! WHAT IS IT?" THEY'LL LOOK YOU RIGHT IN THE EYE AND SAY, "YOU DON'T WANT TO KNOW." YOU KNOW WHAT? I'M SURE THEY'RE RIGHT.

ON SEVERAL OCCASIONS I'VE STARED AT MY PLATE AND ASKED, "IS THIS WHAT YOU WERE TRYING TO CATCH OR THE BAIT YOU WERE TRYING TO CATCH IT WITH?" THEY JUST LAUGH, BUT I AM SERIOUS! JUST BECAUSE IT'S SERVED OVER RICE AND SMELLS GREAT DOESN'T NECESSARILY MEAN THAT GOD INTENDED IT TO BE AN ENTRÉE.

I USED TO USE CRAWFISH AS BAIT AND NOW, NOT ONLY DO I EAT THE TAILS, BUT I WILLINGLY AND EAGERLY SUCK THE JUICE OUT OF THE HEADS AS WELL. I WASN'T RAISED THAT WAY. WHY WOULD I DO SUCH A THING? THERE'S ONLY ONE EXPLANATION — THESE PEOPLE HAVE BRAINWASHED ME. MY STOMACH IS ETERNALLY GRATEFUL.

Chicken Gumbo

*F*or some of my relatives this recipe begins . . .
"Go out in the front yard and catch a chicken." —Jeff

1 chicken
1 cup chocolate Brown Roux (see page 44)
1 large onion, chopped
1 green pepper, chopped
3 stalks celery, cut into 1/2-inch slices
1 clove garlic, crushed and minced
1 pound cooked ham, cut into 1/2-inch cubes
1 pound kielbasa sausage (or smoked sausage) halved lengthwise
and cut into 1/2-inch slices
2 cups okra, cut into 1/2-inch slices
1 16-ounce can crushed tomatoes
1/2 teaspoon salt
1 teaspoon black pepper
1/2 teaspoon Tabasco sauce
2 bay leaves
1 teaspoon oregano
1/2 teaspoon thyme

■ Cover chicken with water and boil until tender. Remove chicken and let cool, debone and cut into bite-size pieces. Continue to boil broth until reduced by half. Reserve.

■ Heat roux in heavy skillet until hot. Add onion, green pepper, celery and garlic and cook for 15 minutes over medium heat.

■ Add remaining ingredients, including chicken, to stockpot. Simmer over low heat for 1 hour. Add broth if additional liquid is needed. Serve over rice.

Serves 8.

Seafood Gumbo

1 cup chocolate Brown Roux (see page 44)
1 large onion, chopped
1 green pepper, chopped
3 stalks celery, cut into 1/2-inch slices
1 clove garlic, crushed and minced
1 pound kielbasa sausage (or smoked sausage), halved lengthwise
and cut into 1/2-inch slices
2 cups okra, cut into 1/2-inch slices
1 16-ounce can crushed tomatoes
1/2 teaspoon salt
1 teaspoon black pepper
1/2 teaspoon Tabasco sauce
2 bay leaves
1 teaspoon oregano
1/2 teaspoon thyme
2 pounds shrimp, peeled and deveined
1 can oysters
1 pound crabmeat
1 pound sea scallops

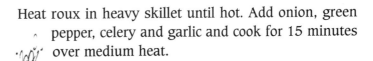

■ Heat roux in heavy skillet until hot. Add onion, green pepper, celery and garlic and cook for 15 minutes over medium heat.

■ Add vegetable/roux mixture and remaining ingredients, except seafood, to stockpot. Simmer over low heat for 1 hour. Add seafood and cook for 20 minutes more on low heat. Add broth if additional liquid is needed. Serve over rice.

SERVES 8.

Making a Roux

The roux is the key to outstanding gumbo and étouffée dishes. It adds a nutty almond flavor to the dish that you can get no other way. Although it is a slow, tedious process, it is worth the trouble. If you make gumbos and roux-type dishes often, you can cook a large batch and store it in the refrigerator for up to 3 months with no reduction in flavor. Simply stir and heat when ready to use.

**1 cup all-purpose flour
1 cup cooking oil**

■ Place flour and oil in heavy skillet and cook over medium heat, stirring constantly, until roux is chocolate brown. This process can take up to an hour. Be very careful not to burn it. When roux begins to brown, it turns quickly. When it reaches the desired color add the chopped vegetables (prepared in advance). This will stop the browning process right where you want it.

Jambalaya

1 small fryer chicken
2 cups chicken broth
1 cup chopped onions
1 cup chopped celery
1/2 cup chopped green pepper
1/2 cup chopped green onions
2 cups long-grain rice
1 pound kielbasa or smoked sausage,
halved lengthwise and cut into 1/4-inch slices
2 tablespoons butter
2 16-ounce cans crushed tomatoes with juice
2 cloves garlic, minced
1 teaspoon black pepper
1 teaspoon salt
1/2 teaspoon red pepper
2 teaspoons oregano
4 bay leaves
2 teaspoons thyme
1/2 teaspoon Tabasco
3 pounds shrimp, peeled and deveined

■ Place chicken and broth in stockpot and cover with water. Add onions, celery, peppers and green onions. Boil chicken until cooked and tender. Remove from stock and let cool; debone and cut into bite-size pieces and return to pot. Add rice to stock and continue to simmer. Sauté sausage in butter for 10 to 15 minutes until lightly browned, add tomatoes, garlic and seasonings and stir thoroughly. Simmer for more 15 minutes. Add shrimp, stir and simmer 10 to 15 minutes or until shrimp are pink. Remove bay leaves and serve.

SERVES 8.

Shrimp Creole

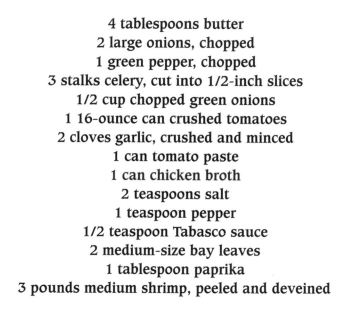

4 tablespoons butter
2 large onions, chopped
1 green pepper, chopped
3 stalks celery, cut into 1/2-inch slices
1/2 cup chopped green onions
1 16-ounce can crushed tomatoes
2 cloves garlic, crushed and minced
1 can tomato paste
1 can chicken broth
2 teaspoons salt
1 teaspoon pepper
1/2 teaspoon Tabasco sauce
2 medium-size bay leaves
1 tablespoon paprika
3 pounds medium shrimp, peeled and deveined

■ Melt butter in heavy pot and sauté vegetables for 10 to 15 minutes, untill tender. Add remaining ingredients and simmer for 30 minutes. Add shrimp and simmer for an additional 20 minutes. Stir occasionally. Serve hot over rice.

SERVES 6.

Crawfish Étouffée

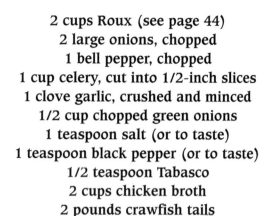

2 cups Roux (see page 44)
2 large onions, chopped
1 bell pepper, chopped
1 cup celery, cut into 1/2-inch slices
1 clove garlic, crushed and minced
1/2 cup chopped green onions
1 teaspoon salt (or to taste)
1 teaspoon black pepper (or to taste)
1/2 teaspoon Tabasco
2 cups chicken broth
2 pounds crawfish tails

■   In a large, heavy skillet, bring roux to medium-high heat and add vegetables. Cook for 15 minutes. Add seasonings and enough broth to bring to desired consistency. Add crawfish tails and simmer for 20 minutes more. Serve over rice.

SERVES 6.

Blackened Fish

Paul Prudhomme created the blackening process and the original dish was blackened redfish. It was such a wonderful dish it spread rapidly throughout the nation and even created a shortage of redfish. When this happened, other types of fish were used, including pompano, red snapper, walleye, salmon, tuna and even catfish.

The blackening process involves very high heat and cannot be done in the house unless you have a jet engine in your vent hood! You must cook this dish outside. Many of the variations of the original process have been used by restaurants but are not the same as that used by Paul Prudhomme, in K-Paul's Restaurant in New Orleans.

1 tablespoon sweet paprika
2 1/2 teaspoons salt
1 teaspoon onion powder
1 teaspoon garlic powder
1 teaspoon ground red pepper
3/4 teaspoon black pepper
1/2 teaspoon dried thyme
1/2 teaspoon oregano
3 sticks unsalted butter,
melted in small skillet and kept warm
6 8- to 10-ounce fillets of fish (at room temperature)

■ Thoroughly combine seasoning ingredients in a small bowl. Set aside.

■ Heat a large cast-iron skillet over very high heat until it is extremely hot, just short of the point at which white ash forms in the bottom of the skillet. Add 1 tablespoon melted butter to the heated skillet. Dip each fish into the reserved butter, coating both sides, then sprinkle with seasoning mixture on both sides. (If you lay fish down to sprinkle be sure surface is warm so butter will not congeal and pull away from fish.) Place fish in hot skillet one at a time. Pour 1 tablespoon of melted butter on top of fish. (Be careful, butter may flame up.) Cook until crust forms on underside (about 2 minutes), turn fish over, pour 1 tablespoon melted butter on top. Cook until just done or about 2 minutes more. Serve while hot. Clean skillet and repeat procedure for each piece. Do not stack cooked fish. Place on a warm plate until ready to serve.

⊙━━━◯ SERVES 6.

Modified from the original recipe by Paul Prudhomme
in Chef Paul Prudhomme's Louisiana Kitchen.

Shrimp Étouffée

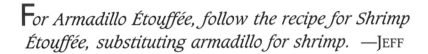

*F*or *Armadillo Étouffée, follow the recipe for Shrimp Étouffée, substituting armadillo for shrimp.* —Jeff

2 cups Roux (see page 44)
2 large onions, chopped
1 bell pepper, chopped
1 cup celery, cut into 1/2-inch slices
1/2 cup chopped green onions
1 clove garlic, crushed and minced
1 teaspoon salt (or to taste)
1 teaspoon black pepper (or to taste)
1/2 teaspoon Tabasco
2 cups chicken broth
2 pounds shrimp, peeled and deveined

■ In a large, heavy skillet, bring roux to medium-high heat and add vegetables. Cook for 15 minutes. Add seasonings and enough broth to bring to desired consistency. Add shrimp and simmer for 20 more minutes more. Serve over rice.

SERVES 6.

FOXWORTHY
FAMILY COOKING

Jennifer's Cranberry Salad

*A*lways save the empty Cool Whip containers —
they make great salad bowls and look
beautiful in any china cabinet. —JEFF

1 large can crushed pineapple
1 cup of ginger ale
1 large package (or 2 small) lemon Jell-O
1 can whole cranberries

TOPPING:
1 8-ounce package cream cheese
1 8-ounce container Cool Whip
1 cup chopped pecans (optional)

■ Drain pineapple juice into a measuring cup and add enough water to make one cup. Heat pineapple juice to boiling. Add ginger ale and mix in Jell-O. Add pineapple and whole cranberries. Stir to mix thoroughly. Pour into 9 x 13-inch casserole and refrigerate to congeal. Once congealed spread on the topping.

■ To make topping, mix cream cheese, Cool Whip and nuts with mixer and gently spread to cover top.

SERVES 8.

Recipe courtesy of
Jennifer Watts,
Tyrone, Georgia

Jay's Boiled Peanuts

This is an old family recipe. Be sure to follow directions carefully. —JEFF

**2 to 5 pounds fresh peanuts off the vine
(do not let dry out, do not shell)
Water to cover
2 tablespoons salt per pound of peanuts**

■ Wash peanuts, cover with water, add salt and boil for 2 hours at slow boil or until tender.

*Recipe courtesy of
Jay Foxworthy,
McDonough, Georgia*

Rhonda's Broccoli & Rice Casserole

2 cans cream of mushroom soup
1 stick butter or margarine
1 tube squeeze-type cheese spread or 1 jar Cheese Whiz
1 cup chopped onion
1 cup chopped celery
2 8-ounce packages frozen chopped broccoli
1 3/4 cups rice

■ Preheat oven to 350 degrees. Heat soup, butter and cheese spread and blend well. Combine soup mixture with remaining ingredients, place in a greased casserole dish and bake for 45 minutes.

SERVES 6.

Recipe courtesy of
Rhonda Foxworthy,
McDonough, Georgia

Jeff's Iced Tea in the Sun

1 gallon water
3 family-size tea bags
1 lemon, cut into slices
1 cup sugar

■ Fill clean gallon jar with water and add remaining ingredients. Place in direct sunlight for about 4 hours. Stir thoroughly, chill and serve.

Jim's Note: *Even though women liberally assign title "Gourmet" to men who cook or at least attempt to (they do this so men will be encouraged to cook more often), neither of my sons will ever receive honorable mention in that category. Both of them had to have help with the complicated recipes they submitted for this book — "Jay's Boiled Peanuts" and "Jeff's Iced Tea in the Sun."*

Jeff's Note: *You can also make Jeff's Iced Tea in the rain. The portion will serve more but the taste is somewhat diluted.*

*Recipe courtesy of
the Number 1
Redneck himself*

Gregg's
New Orleans Special

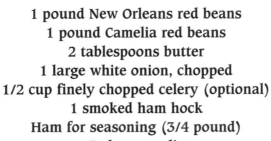

1 pound New Orleans red beans
1 pound Camelia red beans
2 tablespoons butter
1 large white onion, chopped
1/2 cup finely chopped celery (optional)
1 smoked ham hock
Ham for seasoning (3/4 pound)
2 cloves garlic
2 bay leaves
Salt and pepper (to taste)
Sugar

■   After rinsing and sorting, place beans in large heavy pot and cover with water. Soak overnight.

■   In butter, sauté onion and celery with ham pieces until vegetables are clear. Add meat, vegetables and seasonings to beans in pot. Add additional water to cover all. Cover and simmer until beans are cooked through, about 2 hours. Stir beans often and mash against side of pot as they soften to make mixture creamy. Add a pinch of sugar as beans are cooking. Serve over white rice.

SERVES 6 TO 8.

Recipe courtesy of
Gregg Foxworthy,
Alpharetta, Georgia

Paw Paw's Pecan Pie

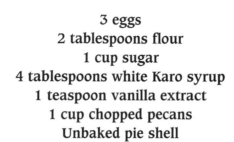

3 eggs
2 tablespoons flour
1 cup sugar
4 tablespoons white Karo syrup
1 teaspoon vanilla extract
1 cup chopped pecans
Unbaked pie shell

■ Preheat oven to 250 degrees. Beat eggs slightly. Add flour, sugar, syrup, vanilla and nuts. Pour mixture into unbaked pie shell and bake for 1 hour or until pie is firm to touch.

Recipe courtesy of
Laura Dixon,
Cumming, Georgia

Aunt Sara's
Fried Chicken

1 chicken (2 1/2 to 5 pounds), cut into pieces
Salt
Pepper
1/2 cup water
1 cup self-rising flour
Cooking oil

■   Rinse chicken and place in a large bowl. Sprinkle with salt and pepper. Pour water into bowl. Using your hands, add flour a little at a time, turning mixture until pieces of chicken are sticky with the flour and water. (Chicken will not be completely covered). Fry until golden brown in skillet or deep fryer heated to 325 degrees for 15 to 18 minutes.

Recipe courtesy of
Sandra Scott,
Denmark, South Carolina
for Sara Abstance

Sandra's Old-Fashioned Hot Milk Cake

(Not to be confused with Modern Hot Milk Cake)

4 eggs
2 cups sugar
2 cups all-purpose flour
2 teaspoons baking powder
1 teaspoon salt
1 stick oleo or butter
1 cup of milk
1 teaspoon vanilla

ICING:
2 cups sugar
1 stick butter or oleo
1/3 cup cocoa
3/4 cup evaporated milk

■ Preheat oven 350 degrees. Grease and flour two cake pans or one
9 x 13-inch pan.

■ Beat eggs and sugar until light and foamy. Add flour, baking powder
and salt. Mix well. Heat oleo and milk to boiling. Add to mixture and stir
slowly until well blended. Add vanilla. Pour in prepared pans. Bake until
golden brown.

■ To make icing, mix all ingredients in heavy saucepan. Bring to boil
over medium heat for 2 minutes. (Watch carefully, it burns easily). Do
not stir. Remove from heat and cool for 10 minutes. Spoon slowly over
layers. Icing may drip. Continue to cover layers until all icing is used. It
will harden as it cools.

Recipe courtesy of
Sandra Scott,
Denmark, South Carolina

Audrey's Catfish Stew

2 to 3 pounds catfish
8 medium potatoes, diced
1/4 pound fatback
1 large onion
Salt & pepper to taste
2 cans evaporated milk
1 small can tomato sauce
6 eggs, boiled and diced

■   Boil catfish in salted water until tender, debone and set aside. Use water from catfish to cook potatoes. Cut fatback in strips and fry in pan. When strips are brown and all grease is out remove fatback. Dice onions and sauté in grease from fatback until tender. Add onion and grease to potatoes and simmer together. Add salt and pepper, catfish, milk, tomato sauce, and boiled eggs. Heat stew but do not allow to boil. Serve with saltines.

■   For a healthier stew, use 1/2 cup canola oil instead of fatback.

SERVES 6.

Recipe courtesy of
Audrey Phillips,
Denmark, South Carolina

Vickie's Lasagna

1 package lasagna noodles
1 large onion, chopped
1 clove garlic, minced, or 1 teaspoon garlic powder
1 1/2 pounds lean ground beef
1 can Italian-style cut tomatoes
1 can Italian-style tomato sauce
2 tablespoons cooking oil
1 teaspoon oregano
1/2 teaspoon basil
Nonstick cooking spray
1 16-ounce container ricotta cheese
2 cups shredded mozzarella cheese
Parmesan cheese

■ Preheat oven to 375 degrees. Cook lasagna noodles according to package directions. While noodles are cooking, sauté onions and garlic in oil in a heavy skillet over medium heat until onion is transparent. Add ground beef and brown, stirring often. Add cut tomatoes, tomato sauce and seasonings. Stir and cook 5 minutes.

■ Spray a 9 x 13-inch lasagna pan with nonstick cooking spray. Place a layer of cooked noodles, then a layer of meat sauce, and then spread half the ricotta cheese onto meat sauce. Repeat and end with a layer of noodles. Top with shredded mozzarella and sprinkle generously with Parmesan cheese. Cover with aluminum foil and bake for 45 minutes or until bubbly. Serve with a salad and Italian bread.

SERVES 6.

Recipe courtesy of
Vicky Abstance,
Denmark, South Carolina

Carole's Green Bean Casserole

2 16-ounce packages frozen french-cut green beans,
thawed and drained

1 10 3/4-ounce can condensed cream of mushroom soup

3/4 cup milk

1 2.8-ounce can french-fried onion rings, separated

1 jar bacon bits

1/8 teaspoon black pepper

■   Preheat oven to 350 degrees. In a bowl, combine beans, soup, milk, 1/2 can of onion rings, 1/2 jar of bacon bits and black pepper. Pour into 1 1/2-quart casserole. Bake 30 minutes. Top with remaining onion rings and bacon bits. Bake 5 minutes longer.

SERVES 6.

Recipe courtesy of
Carole Holten,
Stockbridge, Georgia

Patti's Layer Cookies

1/2 stick margarine, melted
1 cup graham cracker crumbs
1 cup shredded coconut
1 6-ounce package chocolate chips
1 can sweetened condensed milk
1 cup chopped nuts (optional)

■ Preheat oven 325 degrees. Add each ingredient in layers to a 9 x 12-pan. Bake for 30 minutes. Chill before slicing into squares.

Recipe courtesy of
Patti McDonald,
Hilton Head, South Carolina

Aunt Rose's German Chocolate Cake

4 ounces German chocolate
1/2 cup water
4 egg whites
2 cups sugar
2 cups cake flour, sifted
1 teaspoon baking soda
1/4 teaspoon salt
16 tablespoons soft butter
4 egg yolks
1 cup buttermilk
2 teaspoons pure vanilla

GERMAN CHOCOLATE CAKE FROSTING:
12 ounces evaporated milk
4 egg yolks, beaten
1 1/2 cups sugar
12 tablespoons softened butter
2 teaspoons vanilla
2 cups fresh or frozen shredded coconut
1 cup chopped pecans, toasted

■ Preheat oven to 350 degrees. Line three 9-inch cake pans with wax paper.

■ Melt chocolate in water in microwave for approximately 1 minute on high setting, stir and set aside to cool. Beat egg whites until stiff peaks form. Add 1/3 cup sugar and mix thoroughly. Refrigerate until rest of batter is mixed.

■ In a large bowl, combine flour, baking soda and salt, mix well and set aside. In another bowl beat remaining sugar and butter until fluffy (approximately 10 minutes). Add egg yolks, one at a time, beating well after each addition. Add melted chocolate and mix well. Alternately add flour mixture and buttermilk, mixing well. Add vanilla. Fold in egg whites.

■ Divide batter equally into three pans. Bake 30 minutes (until center springs back when touched). Cool in pan for 10 minutes, then continue to cool on cake rack.

■ For frosting, combine milk, egg yolks, sugar and butter in thick-bottomed saucepan. Cook over medium heat until thick (approximately 8 to 12 minutes), stirring continuously with a whisk. Remove from heat. Stir in vanilla, coconut, and nuts. When cake and frosting have cooled, ice middle of each layer, overlapping frosting over edges. Ice edges and top.

SERVES 4.

Recipe courtesy of
Rose McGee,
Hilton Head, South Carolina

Big Jim's Steak Diane

This is a meat that is very simple to prepare,
and if you are of the male gender,
will surely earn you the title "Gourmet" cook.

4 tenderloin fillets 2 to 3-inches thick, butterflied and pounded to
1/4-inch thickness (get the butcher to do this for you)
Meat tenderizer
Garlic powder
Black pepper
Worcestershire sauce
2 tablespoons peanut oil
4 tablespoons butter
Courvoisier
Red wine (use the same wine you serve with the steaks)

VEGETABLES FOR STEAK DIANE:
2 medium onions, quartered
1 pound sliced mushrooms
4 tablespoons butter
2 ounces red wine
1/2 teaspoon salt
1/2 teaspoon garlic powder
1/2 teaspoon black pepper

■ Marinate by sprinkling both sides of each steak with the meat tenderizer, garlic powder and pepper. Sprinkle with Worcestershire and rub into the steak. Refrigerate for 2 to 4 hours.

■ Heat large skillet over high heat and add oil and butter. Cook steaks, one at a time, for 1 1/2 minutes. Turn and cook one minute more. Pour 1 ounce of Courvoisier over and flame. Pour 1 ounce of red wine over. Wait 30 seconds and remove to warm platter in warm oven. Repeat until all steaks are ready. Cook juices in pan until reduced by half and serve over steaks or on the side.

■ To prepare vegetables, sauté onions and mushrooms in butter, add wine and seasonings and serve over steaks or on the side.

SERVES 4.

Minnie's Cushaw Pie

2 cups cooked cushaw
2 cups sugar
3/4 stick of butter or margarine, melted
2 eggs
1 large can evaporated milk
1 tablespoon flour
1 teaspoon nutmeg
1 teaspoon pumpkin pie spice
1 tablespoon vanilla

■ Preheat oven to 350 degrees. Prepare cushaw by removing rind, cutting into cubes and boiling until tender. Drain and cool in a strainer for several minutes. Put drained cushaw in a large bowl and blend with mixer until the lumps are gone. Add sugar and mix well. Add butter to mixture and beat in eggs and milk. In a cup or small bowl mix flour, nutmeg, and pumpkin pie spice, then sift this mixture over batter and stir to blend in. Add vanilla and mix.

■ Pour into 2 unbaked pie shells and bake for about 45 minutes. (A knife inserted in the center will come out clean when done). This can be used as a substitute for Pumpkin Pie if you wish.

*Recipe courtesy of
Minnie Doyle,
Flemingsburg, Kentucky*

Gloria's Roast Beef

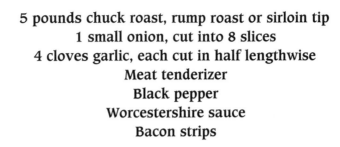

5 pounds chuck roast, rump roast or sirloin tip
1 small onion, cut into 8 slices
4 cloves garlic, each cut in half lengthwise
Meat tenderizer
Black pepper
Worcestershire sauce
Bacon strips

■ Preheat oven to 350 degrees. Make eight 1-inch deep cuts, equally spaced along top of roast. Place a slice of onion in one and a slice of garlic in the next, alternating until all are filled. Sprinkle roast with meat tenderizer and black pepper. Sprinkle with Worcestershire and rub into roast. Place strips of bacon on top. Cook for 20 minutes per pound for medium. Adjust time for rare to well done.

⬤━⬤ SERVES 6.

Recipe courtesy of
Wally Caddell,
Gainesville, Georgia

Melissa's
Tarragon Chicken

6 boneless chicken breasts
1 can cream of mushroom soup
1 cup sour cream
1 small can sliced mushrooms
1/4 cup sherry (optional)
1 tablespoon dried tarragon or 2 teaspoons fresh tarragon, minced

■   Preheat oven to 350 degrees. Rinse chicken breasts and pat dry. Arrange in one layer in large casserole dish. In a medium bowl, mix all remaining ingredients and pour over chicken. Bake for 1 hour. Serve with fluffy white rice.

Serves 6.

Recipe courtesy of
Melissa Foxworthy,
Cumming, Georgia

Scott's Low-Country Boil

Note: *Calculate proportions by allowing for each hearty eater:*

1/2 pound kielbasa sausage, cut into 1-inch pieces
1 tablespoon Old Bay seasoning mix
1/2 pound potatoes, washed and whole
1 onion, cut into eighths
2 ears corn on cob
1/2 pound shrimp, peeled and deveined

■ Boil sausage and seasoning mix in a large pot for 5 minutes. Add potatoes and onions, cover with water and boil 5 minutes. Add corn and boil for 5 more minutes. When all ingredients are done, remove from liquid and add shrimp. Cook 5 minutes or until pink. Serve shrimp in separate bowl or mix all ingredients to serve, draining liquid.

Recipe courtesy of
Scott McDonald,
Hilton Head, South Carolina

Paddy's Vanilla Ice Cream Salad

1 cup hot water
1 3-ounce package Jell-O (any flavor)
1 small to medium can crushed pineapple with juice
1 pint vanilla ice cream
3 bananas, cut very fine

■   Dissolve Jell-O in hot water. Heat Jell-O and pineapple on stove, but be careful not to boil. Pour this over ice cream. When dissolved, add bananas and let sit overnight in refrigerator.

Recipe courtesy of
Paddy Claypool,
Flemingsburg, Kentucky

Aunt Helen's Jeff Davis Pie

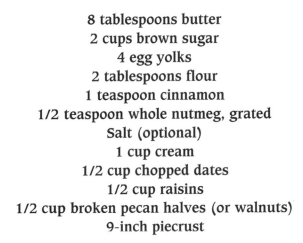

8 tablespoons butter
2 cups brown sugar
4 egg yolks
2 tablespoons flour
1 teaspoon cinnamon
1/2 teaspoon whole nutmeg, grated
Salt (optional)
1 cup cream
1/2 cup chopped dates
1/2 cup raisins
1/2 cup broken pecan halves (or walnuts)
9-inch piecrust

MERINGUE TOPPING:
4 egg whites
1/2 cup sugar

■ Preheat oven to 300 degrees. Cream butter and sugar well and beat in egg yolks one at a time. Sift the flour and spices together, adding a little salt if desired. Blend into the egg mixture until smooth. Gradually blend in the cream. Stir in the fruit and nuts. Bake in 9-inch piecrust for about 40 minutes. Top with meringue.

■ To make meringue topping, beat egg whites while gradually adding sugar until peaks form.

Recipe courtesy of
Minnie Doyle,
Flemingsburg, Kentucky

Miriam's
Corn Pone Delight

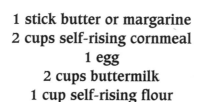

1 stick butter or margarine
2 cups self-rising cornmeal
1 egg
2 cups buttermilk
1 cup self-rising flour
3/4 cup sugar

■   Preheat oven to 425 degrees. Melt butter in bundt pan. Mix remaining ingredients and pour mixture over melted butter. Do not mix. Bake 30 minutes or until done.

Recipe courtesy of
Miriam Doyle,
Flemingsburg, Kentucky

Carla's Peachy Ginger Chicken

Nonstick cooking spray
4 medium boneless, skinless chicken breasts, halved
2 8-ounce cans peach slices
Water
1 teaspoon cornstarch
1 teaspoon grated ginger
1/4 teaspoon salt
4 ounces sliced water chestnuts, drained
2 cups cooked rice

■   Preheat skillet over medium heat. Spray with nonstick cooking spray and add chicken breasts. Cook over medium heat for approximately 10 minutes or until chicken is no longer pink in the center. Remove from skillet and keep warm. Drain peaches, reserving syrup. Add water to syrup to equal 2 cups. Stir in cornstarch, ginger and salt and add mixture to skillet. Cook and stir until bubbling and thickened. Stir in peaches and water chestnuts. Heat thoroughly. Place chicken on 1/2 cup serving of rice. Spoon peach sauce over chicken. Serve with sugar snap peas and glazed baby carrots.

Recipe courtesy of
Carla Doyle,
Flemingsburg, Kentucky

OUTDOOR COOKING– ON THE GRILL/SMOKER

Country Ribs

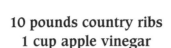

10 pounds country ribs
1 cup apple vinegar

■ In a large roasting pan cover ribs with cold water and add apple vinegar. Let stand at least 4 hours or overnight. Drain and dry ribs and place ribs on smoking racks over medium heat. Cook for 4 hours or until very tender. Turn once during cooking. Dip in barbecue sauce and cook 20 minutes more, turning once. Serve with sauce on the side.

Note: *Once sauce is added, keep ribs on indirect heat. Do not add more wood or charcoal.*

SERVES 10.

Rack of Ribs
on the Grill

4 racks short ribs
1 cup apple vinegar

■ Place ribs in a large pan or bowl with apple vinegar and enough water to cover. Marinate overnight in refrigerator. Remove ribs from marinade and pat dry. Place on smoker or grill rack (indirect heat) and cook for 3 to 4 hours or until tender. (Less time is needed using a grill). Coat with barbecue sauce and cook for another 10 to 15 minutes over indirect heat. Cut up and serve with barbecue sauce on the side.

Note: *Use a rib rack if you have one. It keeps the ribs on their sides so that heat and smoke reach all surfaces. If you don't have a rib rack, connect ribs with skewers and stand them on their sides on the smoker rack. They will cook better. For easier cleanup, place racks of ribs on a jelly-roll sheet to catch drippings. This will not slow cooking time.*

South Carolina Style BBQ Chicken

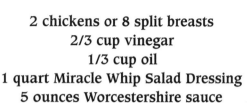

2 chickens or 8 split breasts
2/3 cup vinegar
1/3 cup oil
1 quart Miracle Whip Salad Dressing
5 ounces Worcestershire sauce
1 pint apple cider vinegar
Juice from 12 lemons
3 tablespoons mustard
1/2 cup brown sugar

■ Cook chicken according to instructions (page 94) and baste with mixture of vinegar and oil as the chicken cooks. Mix Miracle Whip, Worcestershire, apple cider vinegar, lemon juice, mustard and brown sugar and simmer for 10 minutes on medium heat. After chicken is done, dip each piece in Miracle Whip sauce. Stack chicken in a large bowl and serve extra sauce on the side.

Note: *This a great variation from the tomato-based barbecue sauce and is really good on chicken. Not suggested for beef or pork.*

Pork Roast

*You might be a redneck if you think the Four Seasons
are onion, pepper, salt and garlic.* —Jeff

1 pork roast (5 to 6 pounds)
Vinegar
Water
Meat tenderizer
Black pepper
Salt
Garlic powder
Worcestershire sauce
Bacon

■ Marinate roast for 4 to 6 hours or overnight in 1 part vinegar and 6
parts water to cover. Remove, pat dry and sprinkle with meat tenderizer,
black pepper, salt, garlic powder and Worcestershire. Cook first on direct
heat to brown on all sides and then transfer to indirect heat until done.
To provide basting, place several slices of raw bacon over roast. The meat
thermometer should read 170 degrees for medium to well done. Remove
roast from heat when thermometer reads 165 degrees, wrap in foil and
let stand in a warm place for about 15 to 20 minutes. If you are timing
the cooking, it should take 30 minutes per pound.

SERVES 6.

Pork Chops

5 pounds pork chops
Vinegar
Water
1 recipe Pork Dry Rub (page 88)

■ Soak pork chops overnight in 1 part vinegar and 8 parts water. Remove chops from liquid and pat dry. Marinate with dry rub and let sit for 2 hours or longer. Cook over direct heat to brown and transfer to indirect heat until done. Cook for about 30 minutes depending on thickness of chops, turning every 7 to 10 minutes. If you want to add barbecue sauce, do so at the end of the cooking process, making sure to cook on indirect heat once sauce is added.

Serves 8.

Smoked Turkey

1 turkey (10 to 20 pounds)
16 tablespoons butter, softened

■ Rub turkey thoroughly with softened butter and place meat thermometer in thickest part of the thigh (being careful that thermometer does not touch bone). Cook over indirect heat at medium-high until thermometer reads 190-195 degrees or until skin on drumsticks has pulled away from the bone and thigh joint moves easily (about 4 to 5 hours).

Salmon on the Grill

1 whole salmon
2 onions, sliced
2 lemons, sliced
1 stick butter, cut into pats
Salt
Lemon pepper
Dill weed
1 ounce white wine
Parsley for garnish

■ Put two or three slices of onion, two or three slices of lemon, and two or three pats of butter in cavity of salmon and sprinkle with salt, lemon pepper and dill weed. Sprinkle outside of salmon on both sides with salt, lemon pepper and dill weed. Place three or four slices of onion, three or four slices of lemon and three pats of butter on surface of a double layer of heavy foil. Place fish on top of these, then place same ingredients on top of salmon. Pour in white wine and seal ends and top of foil. Place on the grill over coals (direct heat). Cook 4 or 5 minutes, turn and cook 4 to 5 minutes more. Remove and let stand a few minutes. Slice into steaks. Serve warm and garnish with lemon slices and parsley.

⟜ SERVES 4.

Hamburgers and Hot Dogs on the Grill

*T*he cheese was my suggestion. —JEFF

2 pounds ground sirloin
1 teaspoon black pepper
1 tablespoon Worcestershire sauce
2 tablespoons minced onion
1/2 teaspoon garlic powder
8 hot dogs
8 slices cheese (optional)
8 hamburger buns
8 hot dog buns
Butter, softened
Garlic powder

■ Mix ground sirloin, black pepper, Worcestershire, minced onion and garlic powder with hands and form into 8 large patties about 1-inch thick. Place on medium-hot grill over direct heat and place hot dogs over indirect heat. Cover grill and cook for 5 to 7 minutes. Turn patties and cook for 5 minutes on other side or until done. Roll hot dogs over and swap ends.

■ If you like cheeseburgers, place a slice of cheese on hamburger patties after turning.

■ Spread buns with soft butter and sprinkle lightly with garlic powder. Bake at 250 degrees until warm. Wrap in aluminum foil before warming if you prefer bread soft. This adds a really good flavor.

Big Jim's "Nasty Dog"

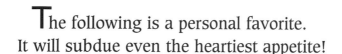

The following is a personal favorite.
It will subdue even the heartiest appetite!

1 large hot dog bun
Chopped onions
1 grilled hot dog
Ketchup
Mustard
Mayonnaise
Sauerkraut
Coleslaw
Chili
Shredded cheddar cheese
Slice jalapeño peppers

■   Fill bun with chopped onions and place grilled hot dog on bun. Top with ketchup, mustard and mayonnaise. Add sauerkraut, slaw and a generous helping of chili to cover. (You will need a fork for this "Dog.") Sprinkle with shredded cheddar cheese and a few slices of jalapeño peppers and dig in!   Be sure to have plenty of your favorite beverage on hand.

Note (from Jeff): *It's also not a bad idea to remove your shirt before eating this.*

Sauces for Barbecue

BASTING SAUCE:
1 cup apple cider vinegar
1 tablespoon cayenne pepper
2 tablespoons honey
1 tablespoon dry mustard
1 tablespoon red pepper flakes
2 tablespoons brown sugar
1 teaspoon Tabasco
1 cup white wine

■   Mix all ingredients and let sit for several days. To control the amount of "heat" in this sauce, add or subtract wine or Tabasco. Use for basting pork or beef while it is cooking. Shake well before use.

BARBECUE SAUCE:
1 cup Kraft Hot Barbecue Sauce
1 cup regular or smoke-flavor barbecue sauce
1 tablespoon Worcestershire sauce
1 tablespoon lemon juice
1/2 teaspoon Tabasco
1/2 teaspoon garlic powder

■   Mix all ingredients thoroughly and use to mop meat at end of cooking or serve on the table. After adding the sauce, keep meat on indirect heat for 5-10 minutes, turn and mop other side and heat for 5 minutes more. Direct heat will cause barbecue sauce to burn and leave a bitter taste in the meat.

Foxy's Barbecue Sauce ("Big Jim" Style)

1 cup apple cider vinegar
1/2 cup brown sugar, packed
2 tablespoons minced onion
2 tablespoons minced garlic
1 can tomato purée
1 tablespoon dry mustard
1 teaspoon cayenne pepper
2 teaspoons paprika
2 tablespoons honey
1 teaspoon chili powder
1/2 cup ketchup
2 tablespoons olive oil
2 tablespoons molasses
1/4 cup white wine
1 tablespoon brandy

■ Mix all ingredients and cook over low heat for 1 to 2 hours. Cool and keep refrigerated. Shake well before using.

Marinades

STEAK AND BEEF ROAST:
■ Sprinkle steaks or roast with meat tenderizer, Accent, black pepper, garlic powder and Worcestershire sauce and rub into meat. Marinate 2 to 24 hours, turning about once per hour.

PORK:
■ Soak pork overnight in vinegar and water (1 part vinegar and 8 parts water). Make sure meat is completely covered.

DRY RUB MARINADE FOR PORK:
Italian dressing
3 tablespoons brown sugar
3 tablespoons paprika
2 tablespoons lemon pepper
2 tablespoons black pepper
2 tablespoons garlic powder
2 tablespoons onion powder

■ Rub meat with Italian dressing. Mix dry ingredients thoroughly and sprinkle generously on pork roast, ribs or pork chops. Let sit for 2 hours then cook on grill.

MARINADE FOR PORK ROAST:
1/2 cup rum
1/4 cup pineapple juice
1/4 cup soy sauce
2 teaspoons mustard
1 tablespoon light molasses or syrup
2 tablespoons lemon juice
2 teaspoon ginger
1 teaspoon garlic powder
1/2 teaspoon black pepper

■ Mix all ingredients and cook over medium heat until reduced by half. Brush over the pork before cooking and baste with mixture during and after cooking.

SPECIAL How-To's

Building a Fire in the Smoker

Cooking a Whole Hog on the Grill

Cooking Chicken on the Grill

Cooking Steaks to Order

Building a Fire in the Smoker

VERTICAL SMOKER:

■ Fill fire pan with charcoal (about 10 pounds) and soak with charcoal starter. Let starter soak in a few minutes then pour on a little more starter and light. Burn until flames go out. Let sit a few more minutes then put pieces of hickory, pecan, mesquite or oak over fire, cover, fill water pans and place meat on the top rack in a single layer or on both racks if there is not enough room on top. Cover and cook for at least 4 hours or until thoroughly done and tender. You may need to add charcoal through the fire door.

CAUTION: DO NOT CLOSE UP SMOKER TOO SOON. MAKE SURE ALL THE CHARCOAL STARTER HAS BURNED AND IT NO LONGER SMELLS BEFORE CLOSING SMOKER.

HORIZONTAL SMOKER:

■ Place about 5 pounds of charcoal in the firebox and sprinkle generously with charcoal lighter. Light and let charcoal burn until coals are hot and gray. Add large pieces of hickory, pecan, mesquite, oak or the wood of your choosing. Let heat to desired level then add meat to smoker grill and cook for 4 hours or more.

CAUTION: TO COOK THE MEAT EVENLY, PLACE IT AS FAR AS POSSIBLE FROM THE FIREBOX AND IN A SINGLE LAYER (MEAT TOO CLOSE TO THE FIREBOX WILL COOK MUCH FASTER THAN THE OTHER PIECES).

Jim's Note: *Put a drip pan in the grill under the meat. It makes cleanup much easier.*

Jeff's Note: *Adding gasoline will make the fire more impressive to your neighbors but tends to taint the taste of the meat.*

Cooking a Whole Hog on the Grill

I grew up in middle Georgia near Sandersville where all real celebrations — political rallies, family reunions, church gatherings, farm bureau functions and anything else that drew a crowd — always included barbecue. In Sandersville, as in all Georgia towns, barbecue meant and still means pork. If it's not identified as something other than pork, it is safe to assume it will be a pig!

At the hunting camp that we ran for a long time we had a whole hog barbecue to celebrate most anything. Some holidays were designated times for a barbecue — like the Forth of July, Labor Day, and Thanksgiving. It was just understood that we would cook a whole hog on those occasions.

These barbecues involved gathering a large supply of good oak and hickory wood and building a big bonfire. We would build a pit by stacking two layers of concrete blocks in a 4 x 8-foot rectangle, leaving a 3-foot gap for coal placement, and putting a steel grid with a 4 x 8 frame over the blocks.

The coals were the real secret for cooking good barbecue. Coals were transferred from the fire to the pit just fast enough to keep a slow drip of grease coming from the roasting pig. That would produce meat that was so tender it would literally fall off the bone and yet be moist and full of flavor. Timing was essential, because if the coals were transferred too fast, the pig would be burned, and if the transfer was made too slowly, the pig would spoil before it cooked. Another key factor was putting the coals in the right place. This was done by placing coals under the thicker cuts of meat in a horizontal "I" pattern, with strings going along the lines of the hams and shoulders and a connecting string along the backbone.

Because it took 15 to 20 hours to cook a 200-pound pig, we had plenty of time to gather everyone around the bonfire and tell lies and drink our favorite drinks. That was the time we were usually entertained by Jeff doing his impersonations of Richard Pryor, Bill Cosby or George Carlin and telling jokes he had either heard or made up. The fainthearted would fall asleep or go home, but those of us with stouter constitutions would rise to the occasion and continue to feed the fire, carry coals, and tell lies. Far into the night, many of the guests underwent startling transformations — they got louder, rowdier and unquenchably thirsty.

About midnight the taste testing would begin with one person after another tearing off a little piece of pork for the purpose of analyzing its progress. By the time our pig was finally judged "done," it was difficult to find three souls stable enough to get real close to the fire, much less lift the hog and carry it into the house. Upon completion of their hazardous mission, the final participants would collapse on (or near) their bunks and not be heard from until noon the next day, when they awoke to a breakfast of spicy barbecue and Brunswick stew.

Cooking Chicken
on the Grill

It is important that poultry be well done. A meat thermometer can be used for larger chickens and turkeys (it should read 185 degrees) but is not very effective with smaller birds. Other methods of checking doneness are:

1. Puncture chicken with a fork at the thickest part of the thigh, if the juices run clear it is done.
2. Move leg up and down, if it moves easily, it is done.
3. Meat should pull away from bone at bottom of leg bone.

The secret to preparing chicken on the grill or in the smoker is to cook it slowly over indirect heat and covered. This will insure that both the white and the slower-cooking dark meat will be cooked evenly and all the way through without being burned. Also, use tongs for handling chicken because punctures cause juices to escape.

ON THE RECTANGULAR GRILL:
■ Open firebox vents, place fire on one end and chicken on the other, close the cover, keep the grill medium-hot and turn chicken every 15 minutes

ON THE ROUND GRILL:
■ Put fire in the center, place chicken around the sides, cover and open bottom and top vents.

Cooking Steaks
to Order

For thick cuts of beef, pork or lamb use a meat thermometer to be certain you cook to the desired stage — 140 degrees for rare, 150 degrees for medium and 160 degrees for well done. If you want to brown the steaks, braise them over high heat and then cook to desired level of doneness uncovered over medium heat.

If you do not use a thermometer, it will take some experience to determine the level of doneness by touch. When the meat is rare, it is very resilient and yields easily to pressure. When well done, meat is very firm. Press on the steak with the side of your spatula and see how it responds. If you do this while it is rare, it will make a deep dent in the meat, but the meat will return to its original form quickly. Do not puncture steak to test as this will allow the juices to escape. Use tongs or spatula to handle steaks and keep the juices sealed inside.

If you are timing the steaks, cook a 1-inch cut for 10 to 12 minutes for medium, and a 2-inch cut for 22 to 25 minutes for medium. Reduce time by about 4 minutes for rare or add about 4 minutes for well done. Turn steaks at least once.

USING A MEAT THERMOMETER:
A meat thermometer takes the guesswork out of cooking meat to the desired level on doneness. Always place the thermometer in the thickest part of the meat away from bone. When temperature indicated is 5 to 10 degrees below the temperature desired, remove meat from oven or smoker. Let meat sit, covered in foil, in a warm place for 15 to 20 minutes. The heat at the center will continue to rise and the juices will move toward the center of the meat.

COMPANY'S COMING– FANCY COOKING

Chicken Cordon Bleu

4 skinned, deboned chicken breasts
4 slices ham
4 slices Swiss cheese
4 tablespoons butter
Salt
Pepper
1/2 cup flour
1/2 teaspoon salt
1/2 teaspoon lemon pepper
1/2 teaspoon garlic powder
1 egg, beaten
2 tablespoons water
1/4 cup cooking oil
1/4 cup butter

■ Beat chicken breasts to 1/4- to 1/2-inch thickness. Place on top of each breast one slice of ham, one slice of cheese and a pat of butter. Sprinkle with salt and pepper and roll by folding in the ends and fastening them with toothpicks. Mix flour, salt, pepper, and garlic powder and roll chicken in mixture. Beat egg and add 2 tablespoons water. Dip chicken in egg mixture and then in flour. Let sit in the refrigerator for 20 minutes or longer. Heat heavy skillet over medium heat and add oil and butter. When butter begins to foam, add chicken. Brown on all sides to a golden brown. Remove from heat and drain on absorbent paper. Remove toothpicks before serving.

Beef Wellington

1 tenderloin of beef (2 to 3 pounds)
Garlic powder
Black pepper
Meat tenderizer
Worcestershire sauce
1 stick butter, plus 4 tablespoons
1 medium onion, finely chopped
1 cup finely chopped mushrooms
2 tablespoons brandy
1 package frozen puff pastry
1 4.5-ounce can liver pâté
2 tablespoons water
1 egg, beaten

GRAVY:
3 tablespoons reserved drippings
3 tablespoons flour
1/2 teaspoon salt
1/2 teaspoon pepper
1 can beef broth
2 tablespoons red wine

■ Trim tenderloin and fold tail over the end to make it a uniform shape. Tie with string.

■ Rub garlic powder, black pepper, meat tenderizer and Worcestershire into meat and place in refrigerator for 2 to 4 hours.

■ Preheat oven to 400 degrees. Melt stick of butter in large heavy skillet and brown tenderloin on all sides. Reserve drippings. Place tenderloin in oven for 25 to 30 minutes. Remove and cool.

■ Sauté onions and mushrooms in 4 tablespoons butter until done (about 5 minutes on medium heat). Add brandy, mix and let cool.

■ Preheat oven to 425 degrees. Defrost pastry and roll out. The pastry should be thin and large enough to cover the tenderloin. Spread paté over pastry, leaving 2 inches on all sides. Spread same area with onion-mushroom mixture. Place tenderloin on pastry topside down. Remove string. Wrap pastry around beef, dampen edges an(and reserve.

■ Mix water and egg and brush pa Place on baking sheet seam side down decorations with reserved dough ai Brush with egg mixture. Bake until pa brown.

■ To make gravy, heat drippings in add flour to make a smooth paste. until flour begins to brown. Add seas and liquids and stir until mixture thickens slightly. Reduce heat to low and stir 3 or 4 minutes. Serve on the side. Makes about 1 1/2 cups gravy.

SERVES 6.

Chicken Curry

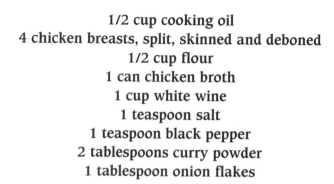

1/2 cup cooking oil
4 chicken breasts, split, skinned and deboned
1/2 cup flour
1 can chicken broth
1 cup white wine
1 teaspoon salt
1 teaspoon black pepper
2 tablespoons curry powder
1 tablespoon onion flakes

■ Add cooking oil to large skillet and heat to medium-hot. Brown breasts and remove. Add flour and stir to form a smooth paste. When flour begins to brown, add remaining ingredients and stir until gravy begins to thicken. Lower heat to simmer and return breasts to skillet. Cover and simmer for 1 hour.

THIS IS A FINE DISH BUT A REALLY GREAT VARIATION IS THE FOLLOWING:

Note: *The 14 boys are the following items. You may use as many as you like but use at least 8 to 10. Prepare a 1/2-cup portion of each.*

14 BOY CURRY
Chopped tomatoes*
Chopped onions*
Chopped mushrooms*
Chopped bananas*
Chopped peanuts or almonds*
Chopped broccoli
Chopped cauliflower
Chopped celery*
Shredded coconut*
Chopped green onions
Chopped apples
Orange chutney*
Shredded carrots
Chopped raisins*

■   Serve rice to guests and encourage them to place a small teaspoon of each of the "Boys" over the rice. Cover all with gravy (see main recipe) and serve one breast to each guest.

THE GUESTS WILL ENJOY ADDING (OR REFUSING TO ADD) THE "BOYS." THE FLAVOR WILL BE A VERY PLEASANT SURPRISE AND WILL CREATE CONVERSATION. THOSE "BOYS" MARKED WITH STARS SHOULD DEFINITELY BE INCLUDED.

Trout Almondine

1/2 cup cornmeal
1 teaspoon salt
4 medium-size brook trout
Salt and pepper
4 sticks butter
1/2 cup slivered almonds
2 lemons, quartered or sliced

■ Mix cornmeal and salt and roll trout in mixture. Cut 2 tablespoons butter into pats. Sprinkle cavity of each trout with salt and pepper and insert a pat of butter. Heat large skillet to medium and melt 1 stick butter. Cook trout until lightly browned and fish flakes easily.

■ In a separate small skillet heated to medium-hot, place 1/4 cup butter and slivered almonds. Sauté gently. Remove trout from pan, place on absorbent paper and then transfer to warm serving dish. Pour sautéed almonds over fish and garnish with lemon quarters or slices.

☞ SERVES 4.

Smoked Fish on the Stove Top

This dish calls for the use of a stove-top smoker but can also be prepared on the grill or smoker.

1 tablespoon wood chips (hickory, pecan, mesquite)
2 tablespoons white wine
4 fish fillets (catfish, perch, bass)
Butter, softened
Salt
Lemon pepper

■ Place chips under inner pan in stove-top smoker and white wine in the bottom of cooking pan. Spread butter over fillets, sprinkle both sides with salt and lemon pepper and place on cooking rack. Place cooker across two top burners of electric stove and cook for 25 minutes until fish is flaky.

The fish can be cooked on the grill or smoker using a seafood screen over indirect heat. This method gives the fish a great flavor.

Fish cooked this way makes great appetizers as well.

SMOKED FISH APPETIZER:
1 smoked fish fillet
1 tablespoon mayonnaise
1 tablespoon chopped sweet pickles
1 teaspoon lemon juice
Ritz or club crackers

■ Mash fish up with fork and stir in other ingredients. Serve as an hors d'oeuvre with crackers.

Note: *Stove-top smokers can be purchased at specialty cookware stores. They make it very easy and efficient to smoke smaller portions of fish, poultry or pork .*

Chicken Kiev

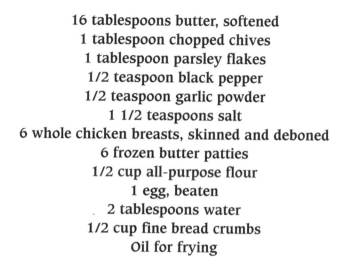

16 tablespoons butter, softened
1 tablespoon chopped chives
1 tablespoon parsley flakes
1/2 teaspoon black pepper
1/2 teaspoon garlic powder
1 1/2 teaspoons salt
6 whole chicken breasts, skinned and deboned
6 frozen butter patties
1/2 cup all-purpose flour
1 egg, beaten
2 tablespoons water
1/2 cup fine bread crumbs
Oil for frying

■ Mix thoroughly butter, chives, parsley, pepper, garlic powder, and 1/2 teaspoon salt. Place in a 1-quart casserole dish and freeze. Cut into six equal pieces (about 3 x 4 inches) and reserve.

■ Cover chicken breasts with wax paper and pound with mallet to a thickness of 1/4 inch. Place a frozen butter patty on each breast. Fold breasts over butter and secure with toothpicks. Mix flour and 1 teaspoon salt and set aside. Mix egg and water in a small bowl and set aside. Spread bread crumbs on a flat surface. Dredge breasts in flour, dip in egg mixture and dredge in breadcrumbs. Let sit until coating dries. Cook breasts in deep fryer at 300 degrees (or heavy skillet with enough oil to cover) for 15 minutes or until golden brown. Drain on absorbent paper, remove toothpicks and serve warm.

Note: *Be careful when you first pierce the breast. You may get a spurt of hot butter.*

Crab Cakes

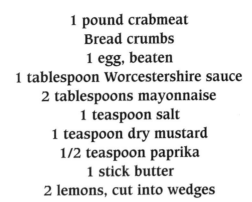

1 pound crabmeat
Bread crumbs
1 egg, beaten
1 tablespoon Worcestershire sauce
2 tablespoons mayonnaise
1 teaspoon salt
1 teaspoon dry mustard
1/2 teaspoon paprika
1 stick butter
2 lemons, cut into wedges

■   Mix crabmeat with 2 tablespoons bread crumbs, egg, Worcestershire, mayonnaise, salt, mustard and paprika until well combined. Roll into 2-inch balls, flatten to 1/2- to 3/4-inch thickness and roll in bread crumbs. Fry in butter until golden brown. Remove to platter with absorbent paper and keep warm while cooking the remaining cakes. Serve with lemon wedges.

⊙⚊◯ SERVES 4.

Veal Oscar

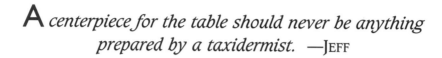

A *centerpiece for the table should never be anything prepared by a taxidermist.* —Jeff

4 veal cutlets
5 tablespoons butter
1 teaspoon salt
1/2 teaspoon pepper
1/2 cup dry white wine
1/2 pound crabmeat
1 tablespoon lemon juice
Cooked asparagus tips

BÉARNAISE SAUCE:
1/4 cup white wine
1/4 cup white vinegar
2 tablespoons minced green onion
1 1/4 teaspoons tarragon
1/4 teaspoon black pepper
3 egg yolks
1 tablespoon warm water
8 tablespoons butter, melted
1/4 teaspoon salt

■ Cook cutlets in 4 tablespoons butter in heavy skillet over medium-high heat until browned. Sprinkle with salt and pepper and add wine. Cover and simmer on medium low heat for about 20 minutes or until tender. Remove cutlets and drain on absorbent paper. Place on platter and keep warm.

■ Cook crabmeat in remaining 1 tablespoon butter and lemon juice for 3 to 4 minutes over medium-low heat and spoon some over each cutlet until all is used. Cover each cutlet with a few cooked asparagus tips and a little Béarnaise sauce. Serve remainder of sauce on the side.

■ To make sauce, mix wine, vinegar, green onion, tarragon, and pepper in a small saucepan and boil until liquid is almost gone.

■ On top of double boiler (over water that is hot, but not boiling) blend yolks with water until creamy. Add melted butter very slowly (1/2 teaspoon at a time) while beating vigorously with a wire whisk. Continue to add butter and beat until all butter is used. Add vinegar mixture and salt and stir. Makes about 3/4 cup of sauce.

Note: *You can buy a Béarnaise sauce mix that is very simple to prepare and almost as good.*

Veal Piccata

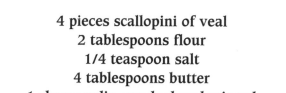

4 pieces scallopini of veal
2 tablespoons flour
1/4 teaspoon salt
4 tablespoons butter
1 clove garlic, crushed and minced
1/4 cup dry vermouth
1 tablespoon lemon juice
4 slices lemon, 1/8-inch thick (for garnish)

■ Pound veal with wooden mallet to 1/8-inch thickness. Dredge in flour and salt mixture. Melt butter in skillet, add garlic and cook until brown. Discard garlic. Place veal in skillet and cook until brown (1 to 2 minutes on each side). Remove to serving dish. Add vermouth and lemon juice to pan and stir, scraping bottom to loosen drippings. Pour over veal; garnish with lemon slices.

SERVES 4.

Stuffed Shrimp

1/4 cup milk
1 egg, beaten
1/2 cup fine bread crumbs
1/2 teaspoon paprika
1/4 teaspoon salt
1 dozen fresh jumbo shrimp, cleaned, deveined and butterflied

STUFFING:
2 slices bacon, cooked and crumbled
1 medium onion, chopped fine
1 stalk celery, chopped fine
1/2 green pepper, chopped fine
1 teaspoon Tabasco
1 teaspoon Worcestershire sauce
1/2 teaspoon salt
1/2 teaspoon black pepper
1 pound crabmeat
1 teaspoon mustard
1/2 cup mayonnaise
2 tablespoons fine bread crumbs
2 tablespoons lemon juice
Butter to baste

■ Preheat oven to 400 degrees. Combine milk and egg in small bowl and mix bread crumbs, paprika and salt in another bowl. Dip shrimp in egg mixture then in bread crumbs and set aside.

■ To make stuffing, cook bacon, remove when crisp and reserve drippings. Chop finely when cooled. Sauté onions, celery and green pepper in bacon drippings. Add remaining ingredients, including bacon. Stir and remove from heat.

■ Place shrimp on greased baking sheet, tails up. Stuff with mixture to overflowing. Baste with butter. Bake for 30 to 40 minutes or until brown.

Serves 6.

SWEETS FOR THE SWEETIE

Homemade Peach Ice Cream

2 cups puréed fresh peaches
1 quart undiluted evaporated milk
2 cups sugar
2 tablespoons lemon juice
Salt (dash)
1 tablespoon vanilla extract

■ Blend all ingredients together and pour into a 1-gallon freezer. Cover and freeze according to freezer instructions. When ice cream is frozen, remove dasher and cover churn with newspapers and let sit for 1 hour.

Key Lime Pie

4 egg, separated
1/2 cup lime juice
1/4 cup water
1 envelope unflavored gelatin
1 cup sugar
1/4 teaspoon salt
1 teaspoon grated lime peel
2 drops green food coloring
1 cup whipping cream
1 9-inch piecrust, baked
Pistachio nuts

■ Beat egg yolks, lime juice and water until blended. Stir into mixture of gelatin, 1/2 cup sugar and salt. Cook over medium heat, stirring constantly until just boiling. Remove from heat. Add 1/2 teaspoon lime peel and coloring, stir and chill in refrigerator until mixture mounds (stir occasionally while chilling).

■ Beat egg whites until soft peaks form and gradually add remaining 1/2 cup sugar. Beat until stiff and fold into gelatin mixture on low speed. Whip cream until stiff and fold into gelatin and egg white mixture. Pour into piecrust and top with pistachio nuts and 1/2 teaspoon lime peel.

Lemon Meringue Pie

FILLING:
3 egg yolks
Juice of 2 lemons
1 can Borden's Sweetened Condensed Milk
1 teaspoon lemon rind (optional)

MERINGUE:
3 egg whites
1/2 teaspoon vanilla extract
1/4 teaspoon cream of tartar
6 tablespoons sugar

FILLING:
■ Preheat oven to 350 degrees. Mix egg yolks and lemon juice thoroughly, add condensed milk and lemon rind if desired and beat. Pour into 9-inch graham cracker piecrust.

MERINGUE:
■ Mix egg whites, vanilla and cream of tartar; beat until soft peaks form. Add sugar gradually until mixture forms stiff peaks. Spread meringue over pie and bake at 350 degrees until meringue is golden (12 to 15 minutes). Chill and serve after pie cools.

German Chocolate Cheese Cake

CRUST:
1 1/2 cups graham cracker crumbs
2 tablespoons sugar
1 teaspoon ground cinnamon
6 tablespoons butter, melted

FILLING:
3 8-ounce bars cream cheese
3/4 cup sugar
1/2 cup sour cream
3 eggs
1 teaspoon vanilla
1 7-ounce package of German sweet chocolate, melted

TOPPING:
6 tablespoons butter
1/2 cup sugar
1/2 cup evaporated milk
2 egg yolks, lightly beaten
1 cup coconut flakes
3/4 cup chopped pecans
1 teaspoon vanilla
Pecans halves to decorate

CRUST:

■ Combine all ingredients and press firmly into bottom and 1/2 to 1 inch up the sides of a 9-inch springform pan.

FILLING:

■ Preheat oven to 350 degrees. Combine cream cheese, sugar and sour cream and beat until smooth. Add eggs one at a time, beating after each addition. Beat in vanilla and melted chocolate and pour into prepared crust in springform pan. Bake for 15 minutes. Lower to 200 degrees and bake for 1 hour and 15 minutes, or until firm in center. Turn oven off, crack door and let cake cool. Run a knife around the edge of the pan and chill, uncovered, overnight.

TOPPING:

■ Melt butter in saucepan and stir in sugar, milk and egg yolks. Cook and stir over low heat until thickened (about 10 minutes). Stir in 3/4 cup coconut, 3/4 cup pecans and vanilla and pour over cake. Decorate with remaining coconut and pecan halves. Chill until ready to serve.

Butternut Cake

1 cup shortening
2 cups sugar
5 eggs
1 cup milk
2 1/2 cups all-purpose flour
1/2 cup self-rising flour
2 to 3 teaspoons butternut flavoring

TOPPING:
1 8-ounce package cream cheese
1 stick margarine
1 box confectioners' sugar
1 to 2 teaspoons butternut flavoring
1 cup chopped pecans

■ Preheat oven to 325 degrees. Cream shortening and sugar for 10 minutes. Add eggs, one at a time, and beat after each addition. Alternate adding milk and flour and beat. Add flavoring. Pour into bundt pan and bake 1 hour at 325 degrees, then 10 to 20 minutes at 350 degrees.

■ To make topping, mix ingredients together. Spread on cooled cake.

Fruit Cobbler

CRUST:
3/4 cup shortening
2 cups flour
1/2 teaspoon salt
2 tablespoons sugar
Ice water

FILLING:
4 cups fruit
(blackberries, raspberries, dewberries, blueberries or peaches)
1 1/4 cups sugar
4 tablespoons flour
4 tablespoons water
2 tablespoons butter

■ Preheat oven to 400 degrees.

■ To make crust, cut shortening into flour and add salt, sugar and enough ice water to make dough hold together. Roll out on a floured board to 1/8-inch thickness and cut into 1/2-inch strips

■ To make filling, wash berries and remove stems and caps. Combine fruit, sugar, flour and water in an ovenproof baking dish. Add short pieces of pastry to mixture and push down. Add remaining strips in latticework fashion to top of dish and dot with butter. Bake until crust is golden brown. You may want to sprinkle sugar on top of crust before baking.

CAUTION: BE SURE TO PREHEAT OVEN TO 400 DEGREES. IF YOU PUT PIE WITH THE SUGAR ON THE TOP IN THE OVEN BEFORE IT IS PREHEATED THE BROILER MAY CAUSE A FIRE.

Apple Pie

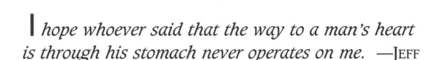

I hope whoever said that the way to a man's heart is through his stomach never operates on me. —JEFF

3/4 cup sugar
6 or 7 cups apples, peeled, cored and sliced
1 teaspoon cinnamon
1 teaspoon lemon juice
2 9-inch piecrusts, unbaked
1 1/2 tablespoons butter

■ Preheat oven to 425 degrees. Mix sugar, apples, cinnamon and lemon juice and pour into 1 crust. Dot top with butter. Form a latticework top with 1/2-inch strips of crust cut from remaining crust. If desired, brush pastry with a mixture of 1 egg white beaten with 2 tablespoons water and sprinkle generously with sugar. Bake for 50 to 60 minutes or until golden brown.

Note: *Place cookie sheet covered with aluminum foil below pie to catch any drippings.*

Berry Pie

1 1/2 cups sugar
1/3 cups all-purpose flour
1/2 teaspoon cinnamon
1 tablespoon lemon juice
4 cups fresh berries
2 piecrusts, unbaked

■ Preheat oven to 425 degrees. Mix all ingredients and pour into a piecrust. Cover with 1/2-inch strips of dough cut from the remaining piecrust. Cook for 40 or 45 minutes or until golden brown.

Note: *Place cookie sheet covered with aluminum foil below pie to catch any drippings.*

Cherry Pie

1 1/2 cups sugar
1/3 cups all-purpose flour
1/2 teaspoon cinnamon
1/2 teaspoon almond flavoring
1 tablespoon lemon juice
4 cups fresh berries
2 piecrusts, unbaked

■ Preheat oven to 425 degrees. Mix all ingredients and pour into a piecrust. Cover with 1/2-inch strips of dough from the remaining piecrust. Cook for 40 or 45 minutes or until golden brown.

Note: *Place cookie sheet covered with aluminum foil below pie to catch any drippings.*

Banana Split Cake

2 cups graham cracker crumbs
3 sticks margarine or butter
2 cups confectioners' sugar
1 teaspoon vanilla
2 eggs
4 large bananas, halved lengthwise
1 20-ounce can crushed pineapple, drained
1 cup fresh strawberries
1 container whipped topping
1/2 cup chopped pecans
Maraschino cherries, halved

■ Mix graham cracker crumbs and 1 stick melted butter and press into bottom and sides of a 13 x 9 x 2-inch baking pan. Beat remaining butter, confectioners' sugar, vanilla and 2 eggs at high speed. Spread over crust. Layer sliced bananas, then pineapple, strawberries, and finally whipped topping onto mixture. Repeat, ending with topping. Sprinkle with pecans and decorate with cherries. Chill at least 4 hours or preferably overnight before serving.

Canteen Cookie Bars

8 tablespoons butter
1 1/2 cups brown sugar
1 cup plus 2 tablespoons sifted all-purpose flour
2 eggs
1 teaspoon sugar
1 teaspoon baking powder
1 cup chopped pecans
1 cup shredded coconut
2 tablespoons lemon juice

■ Preheat oven 350 degrees. Mix thoroughly butter, 1/2 cup brown sugar and 1 cup flour and press into bottom of 13 x 9 x 2-inch pan. Bake 10 minutes.

■ Beat eggs and stir in remaining ingredients. Pour into crust and bake 25 minutes or until golden brown. Cool for 10 minutes before cutting into bars. Makes about 20 bars.

Strawberry Shortcake

1 quart fresh strawberries, cut into halves and quarters
1 cup sugar
1 pound cake, lemon pound cake or package of sweet muffins
Whipped cream

■ Mix strawberries with sugar and let sit at room temperature for 1 to 2 hours. Spoon strawberries over slices of cake, cover with whipped cream and serve.

Gloria's Killer Brownies

1 pound caramels
1 can evaporated milk
1 box German chocolate cake mix
12 tablespoons melted butter
1 cup chopped nuts
1 cup chocolate chips
Confectioners' sugar

■ Preheat oven to 350 degrees. Grease and flour a 9 x 13-inch pan.

■ In double boiler melt caramels in half of the evaporated milk. Set aside. Combine cake mix, melted butter, nuts and remaining evaporated milk. (Mixture will be sticky.) Press half the mixture into bottom of pan and bake for 8 minutes. Remove from oven and sprinkle with chocolate chips. Pour caramel mixture over all and crumble remainder of unbaked dough on top. Bake at 350 degrees for 18 minutes. Sprinkle with confectioners' sugar.

Recipe courtesy
Gloria Caddell,
Cumming, Georgia

Chocolate Chip Cookies

6 tablespoons butter
1 egg
1/4 cup sugar
1 teaspoon vanilla
1/2 cup brown sugar
1 cup flour
1/2 teaspoon salt
1/2 teaspoon baking soda
1 cup chocolate chips
1/2 cup chopped pecans

■ Preheat oven to 375 degrees. Grease a cookie sheet.

■ Beat butter, egg, sugar and vanilla until light and fluffy. Add sugar, flour, salt and baking soda and blend, stir in chips and nuts. Drop on greased cookie sheet 2 inches apart. Bake 8 to 10 minutes.

Carrot Cake

1 cup all-purpose flour
1 1/2 teaspoons baking soda
2 teaspoons baking powder
2 teaspoons cinnamon
1 teaspoon salt
2 cups sugar
4 eggs
1 1/2 cups vegetable oil
4 medium carrots, shredded
1/2 cup chopped pecans
1 can crushed pineapple, drained

FROSTING:
1 8-ounce package cream cheese
1 16-ounce box confectioners' sugar

■ Preheat oven to 350 degrees. Grease and flour a 9 x 13-inch pan.

■ In food processor or mixer, mix together flour, baking soda, baking powder, cinnamon and salt. Set aside. In a separate bowl, mix sugar and eggs until well blended. Add vegetable oil and blend well. Pour oil-egg mixture into the dry ingredients and mix well with a wooden spoon. Stir in carrots, nuts and pineapple, mixing well. Pour batter into the prepared pan and bake 45 minutes. Let cool before frosting.

■ To make frosting, cream together cream cheese and confectioners' sugar.

Coconut Lemon Squares

2 cups self-rising flour
16 tablespoons butter
1/2 cup powdered sugar
4 eggs beaten
1/4 cup fresh lemon juice
2 tablespoons powdered sugar
2 tablespoons granulated sugar

■ Preheat oven to 350 degrees. Mix first three ingredients until thoroughly blended. Press into bottom and sides of greased and floured 12 X 8 1/2 -inch casserole dish. Bake 15 to 20 minutes.

■ Mix remaining ingredients and pour over crust. Bake 15 minutes at 350 degrees. Let cool and cut into squares.

COOKING GAME

Venison Pepper Steak

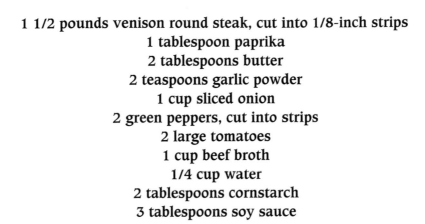

1 1/2 pounds venison round steak, cut into 1/8-inch strips
1 tablespoon paprika
2 tablespoons butter
2 teaspoons garlic powder
1 cup sliced onion
2 green peppers, cut into strips
2 large tomatoes
1 cup beef broth
1/4 cup water
2 tablespoons cornstarch
3 tablespoons soy sauce

■ Sprinkle steak with paprika. Melt butter and add garlic powder, steak, onions, and green peppers, continue cooking until vegetables are tender. Add tomatoes and broth, cover and simmer on low heat about 1 hour. Blend water with cornstarch and soy sauce; stir into steak. Cook until thickened (about 5 minutes). Serve over rice.

Note (from Jeff): *How you acquire the venison is your business. You may hunt or have a friend or relative that does, or you just may have had an unfortunate car accident. No matter. I personally have found that a freezer full of venison takes the sting out of paying your auto insurance deductible.*

SERVES 4.

*Recipe courtesy of
Wally Caddell,
Cumming, Georgia
for Gloria*

Country Fried
Venison Steaks

2 to 3 pounds venison steak, cut into 8-ounce servings
Black pepper
Garlic powder
Meat tenderizer
Worcestershire sauce
1 cup flour
1 teaspoon salt
1 teaspoon garlic powder
1 teaspoon black pepper
16 tablespoons butter
2 cans beef broth

■ Sprinkle each steak with black pepper, garlic powder and meat tenderizer. Sprinkle with Worcestershire and rub in. Marinate for at least 4 hours, turning once per hour.

■ Mix flour, salt, garlic powder and black pepper in a gallon-size freezer bag. Add steaks two at a time and coat well with flour mixture. Let stand for 10 to 20 minutes. Reserve flour mixture.

■ Brown steaks in butter in a large heavy skillet over medium-high heat. Remove browned steaks and add reserved flour mixture. Stir to form a smooth paste. When flour begins to brown add beef broth and stir until gravy begins to thicken. Reduce heat to medium-low, add steaks and simmer for 45 minutes to 1 hour or until tender. Remove to serving platter with gravy on the side. Serve with rice or mashed potatoes.

⌐──◯ SERVES 6.

Venison Nuggets

These nuggets make a great appetizer. People who don't eat venison will eat these swearing they are a good grade of beef. And by the way, they are a favorite of Jeff's. Don't invite him unless you have a big batch!

2 pounds venison steak, cut into 1-inch cubes
1/2 cup vinegar
1 cup plus 4 tablespoons red wine
4 tablespoons Worcestershire sauce
1 small onion, minced
1 tablespoon black pepper
1 tablespoon garlic powder
1 tablespoon meat tenderizer
1 cup flour
1 teaspoon salt

■ Place meat cubes in vinegar, 1 cup red wine, Worcestershire, onion and enough water to cover and refrigerate overnight. Remove and pat dry. Roll in mixture of black pepper, garlic powder, meat tenderizer and 4 tablespoons red wine and let stand 2 to 4 hours.

■ Place flour and salt in gallon-size freezer bag. Add venison and shake until well coated. Let stand 10 to 20 minutes.

■ Cook in deep fat fryer until golden brown. Drain on absorbent paper and serve warm.

Venison Camp Stew
or Deer Goulash

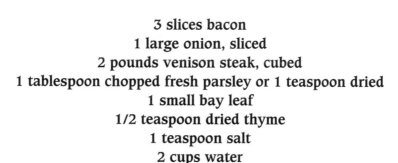

3 slices bacon
1 large onion, sliced
2 pounds venison steak, cubed
1 tablespoon chopped fresh parsley or 1 teaspoon dried
1 small bay leaf
1/2 teaspoon dried thyme
1 teaspoon salt
2 cups water
2 tablespoons flour
Water
1 cup sliced mushrooms
1 cup sour cream

■ Dice bacon and fry with onions until bacon is cooked and onions are glossy. Add meat cubes and seasonings and brown. Add water and simmer 1 to 1 1/2 hours until meat is tender. Mix flour with enough water to form a paste and add mushrooms and paste to stew. Cook 10 minutes, then add sour cream and stir for 1 to 2 minutes. Serve with noodles, salad and red wine.

SERVES 6.

Fried Quail

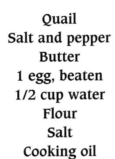

Quail
Salt and pepper
Butter
1 egg, beaten
1/2 cup water
Flour
Salt
Cooking oil

GRAVY:
4 tablespoons grease from skillet
4 tablespoons flour
1 cup milk
Black pepper

■ Split quail, salt and pepper the inside and place a lump of butter in cavity. Combine egg and water. Dredge quail in flour and salt and dip in egg mixture. Let stand for 30 minutes to 1 hour. Heat oil to medium-high and add quail — do not crowd. Brown then reduce heat to medium-low for another 20 minutes. Drain on paper towels. Serve with gravy.

■ To make gravy, in skillet, heat grease and flour and stir with whisk until it begins to brown and become thick. Add milk and stir vigorously, reduce heat, sprinkle with black pepper, stir and serve. Add more milk if gravy is too thick.

Note: *Allow approximately 4 quail per serving.*

Baked Quail

Quail
Salt
Pepper
Butter
Bacon (1 slice per quail)

■   Preheat oven to 350 degrees. Salt and pepper each quail on all sides. Place in a casserole dish, breast side down. Place a pat of butter in each cavity and place half a strip of bacon across the quail and the other half lengthwise. Bake for 30 to 35 minutes.

Note: *Allow 4 quail per serving.*

Barbecued Dove

8 to 10 dove breasts
1/2 cup vinegar
2 cups water
1 1/2 cups white wine
1/2 cup flour
1 teaspoon salt
1 teaspoon paprika
4 tablespoons butter
3 tablespoons peanut oil
1 cup barbecue sauce
1 tablespoon lemon juice

■ Marinate dove in vinegar, water, and 1/2 cup wine for at least 4 hours or overnight.

■ Remove breasts from marinade and pat dry. Mix flour, salt and paprika in a gallon-size freezer bag and add breasts two at a time. Shake to coat thoroughly.

■ Preheat oven to 275 degrees. Mix butter and oil in a hot skillet and brown breasts on all sides. Remove to casserole dish breast side up. Combine barbecue sauce, 1 cup wine and lemon juice and pour over breasts. Bake for 2 hours or until tender. Add more wine if more liquid is needed.

SERVES 4.

Dove in Wine Sauce

8 to 10 dove breasts
Salt
Pepper
8 tablespoons butter
2 cups wine
Water

■ Preheat oven to 275 degrees. Sprinkle breasts with salt and pepper. Melt butter in heavy skillet over medium-high heat and brown breasts on all sides. Remove to casserole dish and add wine and water to cover. Bake for 1 1/2 hours or until tender. Add more water as needed.

■ Reserve juices in casserole dish and pour over breasts in serving dish.

SERVES 4.

Fried Rabbit

2 rabbits, cleaned and quartered
1/2 cup apple cider
1/2 cup red wine
1 cup flour
1 teaspoon salt
1 teaspoon black pepper
1 teaspoon paprika
Cooking oil

GRAVY:
3 to 4 tablespoons pan drippings
2 tablespoons reserved flour mixture
1 cup milk

■ Marinate rabbit overnight in apple cider, red wine and enough water to cover. Remove rabbit from marinade, pat dry and roll in mixture of flour, salt, black pepper and paprika. Let stand for 20 minutes. Add 1 inch of cooking oil to heavy skillet. Heat and add rabbit pieces, being sure not to crowd. Brown on all sides, cover and simmer for 30 minutes. Remove lid and cook for 10 to 15 minutes or until crisp. Remove to absorbent paper and serve with gravy.

■ To make gravy, brown drippings and flour, stirring constantly. Add milk (more than 1 cup if necessary) to obtain proper consistency. Serve on side.

SERVES 6.

Rabbit Stew

*Y*ou *might be a redneck if your neighbors' rabbit disappears and the police question you first.* —JEFF

2 rabbits, dressed and quartered
1/2 cup apple vinegar
1/2 cup red wine
6 potatoes, cut into 1-inch cubes
1 large onion, chopped
2 stalks celery, cut into 1/4-inch slices
1 green pepper, chopped
1 No. 2 can crushed tomatoes
1 can cream-style corn
2 tablespoons salt
1 tablespoon black pepper
1 teaspoon garlic powder
4 tablespoons sugar
1 stick butter
1 cup ketchup
2 tablespoons Worcestershire sauce

■ Marinate rabbit in apple vinegar, red wine and enough water to cover overnight. Remove and pat dry. Place rabbit in stockpot, cover with water and cook until tender. Remove, cool, debone and cut into bite-size pieces.

■ Add potatoes, onion, celery, green peppers, tomatoes and corn to broth and simmer for about 20 minutes. Add remaining ingredients, including rabbit meat, and simmer for 30 minutes. If additional liquid is needed, add water or V-8 juice. Serve hot with corn bread.

⊙━━◯ SERVES 6.

PARTY TIME– FINGER FOODS & DIP

Boiled Shrimp

1 package Zatarain's Crab Boil
3 to 5 pounds medium-large shrimp, in shells

■ Fill large stockpot with 1 gallon (more or less) of water and bring to a boil. Add shrimp boil package and let boil 15 to 20 minutes. Wash and add shrimp. They will sink to the bottom of the pot. As they cook, they will rise to the top and turn pink. Dip them out as they turn pink (only the ones on top) and place in a colander. Immediately run cold water over shrimp to stop the cooking process. Shake and stir shrimp as water runs until cooled. Place shrimp in a small bowl over ice. Shrimp will stay nice and cold. Serve with cocktail sauce on the side.

SERVES 8.

EZ Cheese Dip

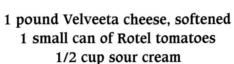

1 pound Velveeta cheese, softened
1 small can of Rotel tomatoes
1/2 cup sour cream
1/2 teaspoon Tabasco

■ Cut Velveeta into 1-inch cubes and melt in microwave. Add other ingredients and mix well. Serve warm with nacho chips. Add cayenne pepper, sliced jalapeño peppers or more Tabasco if you want it hotter.

Firehouse Salsa

If you like Hot Salsa and chips try this:

2 cans crushed or stewed tomatoes with juice
1/2 cup chopped jalepeño peppers
2 large cloves garlic, minced
1 teaspoon salt
1/2 teaspoon black pepper
1/4 teaspoon red pepper
1 cup chopped green onions
1/2 teaspoon Tabasco

■ Mix all ingredients. Put half of mixture in blender and purée. Combine with remaining mixture. Serve with nacho chips.

Note: *The amount of jalepeño peppers can be increased or decreased to get the right level of "hot" to suit. You may want to make two batches — one real hot and one a milder version for your fainthearted friends.*

Bean Dip

If you are planning a lengthy trip in the car with my brother, avoid this recipe at all costs. —Jeff

1 can bean dip
Tabasco
1 green onion, diced
1 tablespoon shredded cheese

■ Add Tabasco to bean dip and mix thoroughly until you have the degree of "hot" you want. Microwave for 30 to 40 seconds to make a warm dip. Top with diced green onions and a little shredded cheese. You may want to make two batches for people who like it really hot and those who like just a little.

Serve with nacho chips.

Sour Cream Dip

1 8-ounce container sour cream
2 tablespoons minced onions
1 tablespoon Worcestershire sauce
2 tablespoons minced green onions
1 tablespoon chives
1/2 teaspoon garlic powder
2 tablespoons white wine (or more if needed)

■   Mix all ingredients thoroughly, chill and serve. If too thick, add more wine. Serve with potato chips.

Hot Spinach Cheese Dip

2 10-ounce packages frozen chopped spinach
4 tablespoons butter
2 tablespoons flour
1 cup milk
1/2 teaspoon black pepper
1/2 teaspoon cayenne pepper
1/2 teaspoon salt
1 tablespoon Worcestershire sauce
1/2 teaspoon Tabasco
1/2 cup diced onions
1/2 pound jalapeño pepper cheese, cut into cubes
1/2 cup Parmesan cheese

■ Cook spinach according to package directions, drain well and set aside.

■ Preheat oven to 350 degrees. Heat heavy skillet to medium heat. Add butter and flour and stir into a smooth paste. Cook 1 to 2 minutes or until flour begins to brown. Add milk, seasonings and onions and stir until mixture begins to thicken. Add cheese cubes and stir until smooth. Add spinach and stir until well mixed. Transfer to a 1 1/2-quart casserole dish. Sprinkle with Parmesan cheese and bake for 25 to 30 minutes. Serve hot with nacho chips or crackers.

Cheese Ball

8 ounces sharp cheddar cheese, shredded
4 ounces cream cheese, softened
2 tablespoons mayonnaise
1/4 teaspoon cayenne pepper
1 tablespoon Worcestershire sauce
2 tablespoons red wine
1/2 cup ground pecans or sliced almonds

■ Mix first six ingredients thoroughly and form into a ball. Roll in nuts. Chill for at least 1 hour. Serve with champagne crackers.

WE FOXWORTHYS HAVE LEARNED THAT WHEN PREPARING FOOD FOR PARTIES, IT'S WISE NOT TO SKIMP ON THE PORTIONS. IN FACT, IF YOUR FAMILY IS LIKE OURS, IT'S PROBABLY IN YOUR BEST INTEREST TO DOUBLE THE SIZE OF THE RECIPES. THAT WAY YOU'LL HAVE ENOUGH TO FEED THE POLICE OFFICERS WHO WILL INEVITABLY SHOW UP AT YOUR FRONT DOOR. MORE THAN ONCE A CHEESE BALL AND SOME CHICKEN WINGS HAVE KEPT MY LOVED ONES OUT OF JAIL.

Sweet Spiced Nuts

1 cup almonds
1 cup cashews
1 cup pecan halves or 1 cup mixed nuts, unsalted
2 egg whites, beaten but not stiff
1/2 cup fine granulated sugar
1/2 teaspoon cinnamon
1/4 teaspoon nutmeg
1/8 teaspoon allspice
1/8 cup brown sugar

■ Preheat oven to 325 degrees. Combine nuts in a medium bowl and add egg whites. Toss until nuts are well coated. Combine remaining ingredients in a separate bowl and roll nuts in mixture. Spread in one layer on baking sheet lined with brown paper. Roast nuts for 25 minutes, shaking pan occasionally. Cool and store in an airtight container in refrigerator. Makes 3 cups.

Hot and Spicy Party Mix

1 stick butter, melted
2 tablespoons Worcestershire sauce
1/4 teaspoon garlic powder
1/2 teaspoon Tabasco
1/2 teaspoon red pepper (cayenne)
1/2 teaspoon celery salt
1 cup Wheat Chex
1 cup Rice Chex
1 cup Corn Chex
1 cup pretzels
1 cup mixed salted nuts
1 cup goldfish crackers

■ Preheat oven to 250 degrees. Melt butter and mix with next five ingredients. Combine remaining ingredients, pour butter mixture over dry mixture and toss until thoroughly combined. Spread in a jelly-roll pan and bake for 30 minutes. Stir at least every 10 minutes. Makes about 6 1/2 to 7 cups. Cool and store in an airtight container. Terrific served with cheese cubes and fruit.

Chicken Wings (HOT)

2 pounds chicken wings
1/2 cup all-purpose flour
1 teaspoon salt
1/2 teaspoon garlic powder
1/2 teaspoon black pepper
1/2 teaspoon red pepper
Vegetable oil

SAUCE:
2 tablespoons lemon juice
2 tablespoons vinegar
2 tablespoons ketchup
1 tablespoon mayonnaise
1 tablespoon mustard
1 teaspoon salt
1 teaspoon Tabasco
1/2 teaspoon cayenne pepper
2 tablespoons white wine

■ Clean wings and clip off tips. Place all ingredients except chicken into a gallon-size freezer bag and shake to combine. Add chicken wings a few at a time. Coat well and remove. Let stand for 10 to 20 minutes. Add about 1 inch oil to heavy skillet and heat to medium-high (325 to 350 degrees). Add wings and brown to a golden brown.

■ To make sauce, mix sauce ingredients and heat sauce in microwave. Dip wings in sauce and serve. Great with carrot and celery strips served with blue cheese or ranch dressing.

Cheese Straws

2 sticks butter
2 cups flour
1/2 pound sharp cheddar cheese, grated
1/2 teaspoon salt
1/2 teaspoon cayenne pepper
2 cups Rice Krispies
Paprika

■ Preheat oven to 325 degrees. Combine first five ingredients and mix by hand until soft. Add Rice Krispies and mix. Roll into balls the size of hickory nuts. Flatten with fork dipped in cold water. Sprinkle with paprika. Bake for 10 to 15 minutes or until golden brown. Yields 35 to 40 cheese straws.

Cheese Tray

One pound of two or more kinds of cheese,
cut into 3/4-inch cubes and served on tray with fruit.

TYPES OF CHEESE THAT MIGHT BE USED ARE:
Cheddar (Sharp or mild)
Colby
Swiss
Muenster
Gruyére
Brie
Monterey Jack
Pepper cheese
Provolone

■ Serve with a variety of crackers and stuffed green olives. Cheeses are always a favorite and are appropriate with any beverage. And so easy to prepare!

Party Fruit Tray

1 cup fresh strawberries, with stems removed
3 bananas, sliced
3 apples peeled, cored and sliced into 1/2-inch wedges
1 pound seedless green or red grapes, in small bunches
1 cantaloupe, peeled and cut into 1-inch pieces
4 peaches, cut into 1/2-inch wedges
3 oranges, peeled and cut into bite-size pieces

■   Arrange on a pretty serving platter around dip or in a watermelon boat.

FRUIT DIP:
1 container strawberry yogurt
2 tablespoons sugar
1/2 teaspoon cinnamon
1/2 cup orange marmalade
1 3-ounce package cream cheese
1/4 cup milk

■   Mix all ingredients well and chill for at least 1 hour. Makes approximately 2 1/2 cups. Add more milk if dip is too thick.

Pizza Squares

1 loaf thick-sliced sandwich bread
1 10 1/4-ounce can marinara sauce
1/2 cup grated mozzarella cheese
1/2 cup grated sharp cheddar cheese
1 small package sliced pepperoni

■ Cut rounds from bread with a biscuit cutter and toast until lightly browned. Spread marinara sauce over each piece of toast and sprinkle with cheeses. Cover each slice with four slices of pepperoni. Broil 4 to 5 inches from heat for 2 to 3 minutes or until cheese browns slightly. Serve warm.

Party Vegetable Dip

1 cup mayonnaise
1 8-ounce package cream cheese
1 8-ounce package sour cream
1 tablespoon Worcestershire sauce
1 tablespoon Tabasco
1 teaspoon salt
1 teaspoon dry mustard
1/2 teaspoon garlic powder
1/2 teaspoon black pepper
1/2 teaspoon celery seeds

■ Combine all ingredients, mix well and chill until ready to serve (at least 1 hour). Yields 3 1/2 cups.

RAW VEGETABLES TO USE:
Celery, cut into 3-inch strips
Carrots, cut into 1/4-inch strips 2 to 3 inches long
Cauliflower florets
Broccoli florets
Zucchini, sliced 1/4-inch thick
Squash, sliced 1/4-inch thick
Radishes, whole or cut into slices
Cucumbers, sliced 1/8-inch thick
Green onions, cut into 3-inch lengths
Green peppers, cut into 1/4-inch strips
Mushrooms, cut into 1/8-inch slices

Vegetable Fritters

BASIC FRITTER BATTER:
1 1/2 cups sifted all-purpose flour
1 teaspoon salt
1 teaspoon paprika
1/2 teaspoon black pepper
1 teaspoon garlic powder
2 tablespoons oil
1 egg, beaten

■ Mix all ingredients and add cold water to make a fairly thick batter. If batter does not stick to vegetables, add more water (a tablespoon at a time). Dip vegetable pieces into batter and drop into hot oil (deep enough to cover). Brown, turn and brown other side. Remove and drain. Place in baking pan lined with absorbent paper and keep in warm oven until ready to serve.

YOU CAN USE ONE OR MORE OF THESE VEGETABLES:
Mushrooms, with stems removed
Zucchini, sliced 1/4-inch thick
Cauliflower florets
Onions, sliced and separated into rings
Squash, sliced 1/4-inch thick

Zucchini Fritters

1 cup flour
1 cup milk
1 teaspoon baking powder
3 eggs, beaten
1/2 teaspoon pepper
1/2 teaspoon salt
1/2 teaspoon paprika
Vegetable oil
1 zucchini, grated

■ Mix all ingredients thoroughly. Drop by the tablespoonful into vegetable oil heated to medium-high. Brown and drain. Serve warm.

Note: *For corn fritters, substitute 1 can whole kernel corn (drained) for zucchini.*

Tuna and Cheese Canapés

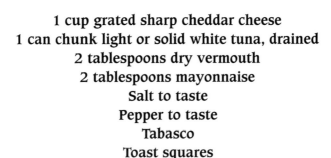

1 cup grated sharp cheddar cheese
1 can chunk light or solid white tuna, drained
2 tablespoons dry vermouth
2 tablespoons mayonnaise
Salt to taste
Pepper to taste
Tabasco
Toast squares

■ Preheat oven to 350 degrees. Combine first seven ingredients and mix thoroughly. Spread on toast squares and bake for about 5 minutes. Serve warm.

TOAST SQUARES:
■ Brush your favorite type of sliced loaf bread with melted butter or margarine and toast in oven until lightly browned. Trim edges and cut into squares.

Water Chestnuts Wrapped in Bacon

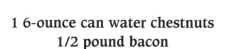

1 6-ounce can water chestnuts
1/2 pound bacon
2 tablespoons Worcestershire sauce
2 tablespoons dry sherry

■ Preheat oven to 350 degrees. Wrap each water chestnut in 1/2 slice of bacon and fasten with toothpick. Place in ovenproof dish and brush with mixture of Worcestershire sauce and sherry. Bake for 15 minutes or until bacon is crisp. Brush again with mixture at about 10 minutes baking time. Serve warm.

Jalapeño Pepper Treats

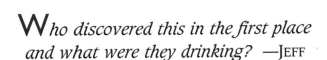

*W*ho discovered this in the first place
and what were they drinking? —Jeff

Ritz crackers
Crunchy peanut butter
1/2 pound bacon, fried and broken into 1-inch pieces
1 jar jalapeño pepper jelly

■   Layer peanut butter, bacon and pepper jelly on crackers. Unusual and
very good!

Stuffed Mushrooms

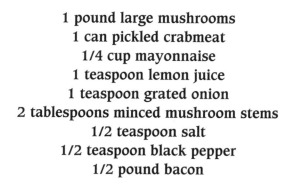

1 pound large mushrooms
1 can pickled crabmeat
1/4 cup mayonnaise
1 teaspoon lemon juice
1 teaspoon grated onion
2 tablespoons minced mushroom stems
1/2 teaspoon salt
1/2 teaspoon black pepper
1/2 pound bacon

■ Preheat oven to 350 degrees. Brush mushrooms clean with mushroom brush or wipe with soft cloth. (Do not wash — mushrooms quickly absorb water). Remove stems, mince and reserve. In a large bowl mix crabmeat, mayonnaise, lemon juice, onion, minced mushroom stems, salt and black pepper. Fill cavities of mushrooms with mixture. Wrap with half a slice of bacon and fasten with a toothpick. Place on cookie sheet and bake for 15 to 20 minutes or until bacon is crisp. Remove and place on absorbent paper. Serve warm.

BREAKFAST IN THE COUNTRY

Basic Grits

3 cups water
1 teaspoon salt
1 cup grits
1 cup milk
2 tablespoons butter

■   Boil water, add salt and grits and stir. Cover and boil 3 minutes. Reduce heat to low and simmer. Add milk to achieve proper consistency. Add butter, stir and serve.

Note: *Grits are better when they cook longer. Just add milk periodically to keep the consistency you want.*

SERVES 6.

Cheese Grits

2 **eggs**
1 **recipe of Basic Grits (see page 162)**
1/2 **cup grated sharp cheddar cheese**

■   Beat eggs thoroughly. Dip out a ladle of grits and mix with eggs, stirring thoroughly. Transfer egg and grits mixture to grits pot. Add grated cheese just before serving and stir well until cheese is melted. Serve hot!

Note: *You can control the consistency by adding milk as you cook.*

⊙━◯ SERVES 6.

Grits Casserole

1 recipe Cheese Grits (see page 163)
4 tablespoons butter
1/2 teaspoon garlic powder
2 dashes of Tabasco sauce

■ Preheat oven to 350 degrees. Combine ingredients and place in a 1-quart casserole dish. Bake for 1 hour.

SERVES 4 TO 6.

Basic Pancakes

1 cup all-purpose flour
1 teaspoon baking powder
1/2 teaspoon salt
2 teaspoons sugar
1 egg, beaten
1 cup milk
1 tablespoon cooking oil

■ Mix dry ingredients in one bowl and egg, milk and cooking oil in another. Add egg mixture to dry ingredients and stir to mix thoroughly. With a large serving spoon drop batter onto hot, greased griddle or heavy skillet. Cook until edges are dry and bubbles form in pancake. Turn and cook until light brown. Stack and hold in warm oven until all are cooked. Serve with butter and syrup or preserves. Try sour cream instead of butter for a tasty change.

Note: *The Basic Pancake recipe found on the Bisquick box is also very good and a little faster to prepare.*

VARIATIONS:
AMARETTO PANCAKES:
■ Add 1 tablespoon of Amaretto liqueur to batter and mix well. It gives excellent flavor.

PECAN PANCAKES:
■ Add 1/4 cup chopped pecans to batter and mix well.

TOPPINGS:
For a tasty alternative to butter and syrup, try serving your pancakes with one of the following combinations: (1) preserves or fresh fruit and whipped cream, (2) peanut butter and syrup and (3) sour cream and syrup (this reduces the sweet taste).

SERVES 4.

Omelet

3 eggs
1 tablespoon cold water
2 shakes salt
1 shake black pepper
1 tablespoon butter

■   Break eggs into a small bowl, add other ingredients except butter and beat just enough to mix thoroughly.

■   Heat omelet pan over medium heat, add butter and tilt pan to coat bottom of pan and 1/2 inch up the sides. Pour in egg mixture and let sit. While cooking, pull egg away from sides of the pan and tilt pan until the uncooked egg runs to the sides. Cook until the eggs are set but moist in the middle. Continue to shake pan a little longer until omelet slides freely in the pan. Lift pan and tilt away from you. Fold omelet with a spatula and slide onto warm plate.

Note: *It is important that the pan be heated before adding the butter. This will prevent the omelet from sticking.*

VARIATIONS:
CHEESE OMELET:
■   Grate sharp cheddar cheese and sprinkle over omelet before folding and serving.

HAM AND CHEESE OMELET:
■ Spread cubed ham down the center of the omelet, sprinkle with cheddar cheese, fold and serve.

STEAK AND ONIONS OMELET:
■Sauté chopped onions, chopped mushrooms and cubed steak in butter until well heated. Add three tablespoons of mixture to the center of omelet, sprinkle with shredded cheese, fold and serve.

CHEESE, ONIONS AND MUSHROOMS OMELET:
■ Sauté chopped mushrooms and onions in butter. Add 2 tablespoons of the mixture down the center of omelet, sprinkle with shredded cheese, fold and serve.

WESTERN OMELET:
■ Sauté green peppers, chopped onions, chopped tomatoes, chopped celery and chopped cooked ham in butter. Add 3 tablespoons down the center of the omelet, sprinkle with shredded cheese, fold and serve.

BACON, MUSHROOMS AND ONIONS OMELET:
■ Cook bacon and sauté mushrooms in bacon grease. Add 2 to 3 tablespoons to center of omelet, sprinkle with cheese, fold and serve.

Basic Crepes Recipe

This recipe can be used for dessert or regular crepes.

3 eggs, beaten
1/2 cup milk
1/2 cup Bisquick
1 teaspoon sugar
Butter

■ Combine eggs and milk and, using a whisk, beat in mixture of Bisquick and sugar. Batter should be thin. Add 1 tablespoon butter to an 8-inch frying or crepe pan and heat until butter bubbles. Pour in just enough batter to make a thin layer over the bottom of pan, tilting pan to make batter cover all areas. Cook until lightly browned. Turn and brown other side. Add another pat of butter and repeat process. The first one always looks bad, but the rest will be nice. Fill each crepe with the filling and roll up.

FILLINGS FOR BREAKFAST CREPES:
1. Spread strawberry preserves over crepes and place a spoon of sour cream down center and roll up. Great for breakfast!

2. Spread with orange marmalade and top with whipped cream.

3. Mix peanut butter and honey; sprinkle with shredded sharp cheddar cheese.

4. Cover with mixture of scrambled eggs and cream cheese and minced green onions.

SERVES 4.

OTHER COOKING WE ENJOY

Gloria's
Spaghetti Sauce

2 tablespoons olive oil
2 cloves garlic, minced
1 large onion, chopped
2 cups chopped celery
1 cup chopped mushrooms
1 to 2 pounds lean ground beef
1/2 teaspoon garlic powder
3 teaspoons salt
2 teaspoons basil
1/4 teaspoon paprika
2 cans (1 pound 12-ounce size) crushed tomatoes with juice
1 12-ounce can tomato paste
1 12-ounce can tomato sauce
1 can beef broth
Red wine

■ Sauté garlic, onion, celery and mushrooms in olive oil for 5 minutes. Add ground beef and brown. Season with garlic powder, salt, basil and paprika. In a large pot, combine crushed tomatoes, tomato paste, tomato sauce and beef broth. Add meat and vegetable mixture and simmer on low heat for about 4 hours. Add a little red wine to bring to right consistency about 10 minutes before cooking is finished.

■ Serve over hot spaghetti noodles prepared according to package instructions.

SERVES 6.

*Recipe courtesy of
Gloria Caddell,
Cumming, Georgia*

Spaghetti & Meatballs

4 tablespoons olive oil, vegetable oil or butter
1 large onion, chopped
1 clove garlic, minced
1 green pepper, diced
1 cup chopped mushrooms
1/2 pound Italian sausage
1/2 pound lean ground beef
1 large can crushed tomatoes with juice
1 6-ounce can tomato paste
1/2 cup red wine
2 bay leaves
1 teaspoon salt
1/2 teaspoon black pepper
1/2 teaspoon thyme
1/2 teaspoon oregano

■ Sauté onions, garlic, pepper and mushrooms in oil over medium-hot heat. Mix meats together and form into 1-inch balls. Add meatballs to skillet and brown. Add remaining ingredients and simmer for 1 hour. Remove bay leaf.

■ Cook spaghetti according to instructions, drain and add melted butter and toss. Serve sauce and meatballs over spaghetti and sprinkle with grated Parmesan cheese.

SERVES 6.

Chicken Cacciatore in the Crock-Pot

1 whole chicken
1 large onion, chopped (Vidalia or Texas sweet preferred)
2 stalks celery, cut into 1/4-inch slices
1 green pepper, diced
1 cup sliced mushrooms
1 can crushed tomatoes with juice
1 small can tomato purée
1/2 cup white wine
1 teaspoon salt
1 teaspoon oregano
1/2 teaspoon black pepper
1/2 teaspoon garlic powder
Chicken broth

■ Cook chicken in salty water until tender. Debone, skin and cut into bite-size pieces. Reduce broth by half and reserve. Add raw vegetables to Crock-Pot first, then add chicken, then other ingredients. Add enough reserved chicken broth to cover and let cook on slow heat for about 8 hours. Add broth if needed. Serve with spaghetti noodles or rice.

SERVES 6.

Sauerbraten

1 5-pound beef rump roast
2 medium onions, sliced
2 cups wine vinegar
2 cups hot water or enough to cover roast
6 whole cloves garlic
4 peppercorns
2 bay leaves
1/2 cup cooking oil
2 cups boiling water
10 gingersnaps

GRAVY:
Strained juices from Dutch oven
1/2 cup sour cream
1 tablespoon flour

■ Put roast in a bowl and add next six ingredients. Marinate in refrigerator for 1 to 4 days. Remove and reserve at least 1 cup of marinade (strained).

■ Add oil to a large heavy Dutch oven and brown roast on all sides. Add boiling water and gingersnaps and simmer covered for 1 1/2 to 2 hours, turning often. Add reserved marinade and simmer for another 1 1/2 to 2 hours. Remove from heat and keep warm in oven.

■ To make gravy, strain juices from the Dutch oven into a medium saucepan over medium heat. Mix sour cream and flour and stir into pan drippings until sauce thickens. Slice meat into 1/4- to 1/2-inch slices and cover with gravy, reserving some for serving on the side. Serve with mashed potatoes.

SERVES 8.

Boliche

1 eye of round roast (3 to 4 pounds)
1 chorizo sausage, chopped
1 onion, chopped
3 tablespoons minced green pepper
1 teaspoon Worcestershire sauce, plus 1 tablespoon
4 cloves garlic, peeled and minced
1 1/2 teaspoons salt
1 teaspoon black pepper
2 large onions, thinly sliced
4 bay leaves
2 cups unsweetened orange juice
1 cup dry white wine
1/2 teaspoon oregano
3 tablespoons bacon drippings

GRAVY:
Roast drippings
2 tablespoons flour
1/2 teaspoon salt
1/2 teaspoon black pepper

■ Cut a pocket lengthwise in center of roast about 1 inch in diameter. Mix sausage, onion, green pepper, 1 teaspoon Worcestershire, 1 clove of garlic, 1/2 teaspoon salt and 1/2 teaspoon black pepper and stuff roast with mixture, packing well. Place half of the onion slices then the roast in the bottom of a large bowl, mix bay leaves, remaining garlic, orange juice, remaining 1 teaspoon salt, white wine, remaining 1/2 teaspoon black pepper, oregano and 1 tablespoon Worcestershire and pour over roast. Cover with remaining onion slices. Marinate in refrigerator for 12 to 48 hours. Remove roast, pat dry and reserve marinade. Heat bacon drippings in a large heavy skillet and brown the roast on all sides. Transfer roast to Dutch oven and pour marinade over. Bring to boil, reduce heat and simmer for 4 hours, basting regularly. If more liquid is needed add wine. Remove roast and let stand for 10 to 15 minutes before slicing. Serve with gravy.

■ To make gravy, heat 1 cup roast drippings to medium heat, add flour and seasonings and stir until it begins to thicken. Add another cup (or a little more if needed) of drippings and stir thoroughly until it is the right consistency.

⊸ SERVES 6.

Pizza

2 cans refrigerated pizza dough
1 pound hot Italian Sausage
1 pound ground chuck
Salt, pepper, garlic powder to taste
1/2 cup fresh mushrooms, sliced
1 large onion, sliced into rings
1 large green pepper, sliced into rings
1/2 pound shredded mozzarella cheese
1/2 pound shredded sharp cheddar cheese
Salt, pepper, garlic powder to taste
1 large jar of Italian mushroom pesto or pizza sauce
1 package sliced pepperoni

■ Roll out refrigerated pizza dough and shape to fit two large, deep-dish pizza pans. Prebake crust according to package directions. Set aside.

■ Preheat oven to 400 degrees. Brown sausage in skillet. Remove and set aside. Brown ground chuck, adding salt, pepper and garlic powder to taste. Remove and set aside. Sauté vegetables in grease remaining in pan (adding a little oil if needed) until done. Season with salt, pepper and garlic powder to taste.

■ Spread pesto or Pizza sauce over prebaked crust. Sprinkle with half the shredded cheeses, then the cooked sausage, then cooked ground chuck, then vegetables. Add pepperoni slices and sprinkle remaining shredded cheeses over all. Bake until cheese is melted and crust around sides is a golden brown.

■ Slice and serve hot with Parmesan cheese and red pepper flakes on the side.

Makes 2 large pizzas; ⌐⊃ SERVES 12.

Fried Rice

1/2 cup peanut oil
1/2 cup sliced water chestnuts
1/2 cup green onions, cut into 1/2-inch slices
1/2 cup chopped onions
1/2 cup chopped celery
4 eggs, beaten
3 cups cooked rice
1 teaspoon salt
1 teaspoon black pepper
1 tablespoon hoisin sauce
3 tablespoons soy sauce

■ Cook vegetables in oil 3 to 5 minutes, stirring vigorously. Push mixture to side of pan, pour in eggs and let cook until done, chop into small pieces with spatula and mix with other ingredients. Add rice, meat (see variations below) and seasonings and stir until heated through. Serve.

SERVES 6.

VARIATIONS:
SHRIMP FRIED RICE:
■ Clean, peel and devein shrimp and add when rice is added.

CHICKEN FRIED RICE:
■ Boil chicken in salty water, skin, debone and chop into bite-size pieces. Add chicken with rice plus 1/2 cup slivered almonds.

PORK FRIED RICE:
■ Cut 1 pound of pork into 1/2-inch cubes and brown before adding vegetables to peanut oil. Add 1 teaspoon dry mustard.

BEEF FRIED RICE:
■ Cut 1 pound lean steak into 1/3-inch strips and sauté in peanut oil before adding vegetables. Add an additional tablespoon of hoisin sauce.

PMS Stew
(Poor Man's Stew)

1 whole chicken
1 stick butter
2 large onions, chopped
1 green pepper, chopped
2 cups okra, sliced
1 pound chopped fresh mushrooms
4 cups cooked rice
1 16-ounce can tomato sauce
1 cup red wine (your favorite)
2 pounds Polish sausage, quartered and cut into 1/2-inch slices
1/2 teaspoon garlic powder
1/2 teaspoon black pepper
1 teaspoon salt
1/2 teaspoon Tabasco (or to taste)
2 tablespoons Worcestershire sauce
1/2 teaspoon oregano

■   Boil chicken in salty water until done. Remove chicken and continue to cook broth until reduced by half and reserve. Remove chicken from bone and cut into 1/2-inch cubes. Sauté onions, peppers, okra and mushrooms in butter. Add chicken and sautéed vegetables to the chicken broth. Add remaining ingredients and simmer 2 to 3 hours. If additional liquids are needed, add chicken broth or Mr. & Mrs. T's Bloody Mary Mix. Serve hot with corn bread.

⌐◯ SERVES 8.

Chili

2 pounds lean ground meat
2 pounds round steak, cut into 1/2-inch cubes
Cooking oil
2 large onions, diced
2 green peppers, diced
6 chili peppers, minced
4 cans crushed tomatoes with juice
2 cans beef bouillon
4 cans red kidney beans with juice
4 tablespoons dark brown sugar
4 tablespoons Worcestershire sauce
1 teaspoon Tabasco
2 tablespoons chili powder
2 teaspoons salt
2 teaspoons black pepper
8 Hershey kisses
1 tablespoon dry mustard
2 teaspoons oregano

■ Brown meat in cooking oil, then sauté onions and peppers in same skillet. Add to stockpot along with the remaining ingredients. Simmer over low heat until meat is tender (1 1/2 to 2 hours). Serve in soup bowls with club crackers and sprinkle with sharp shredded cheese. Better the next day when reheated.

SERVES 8.

Note: *If more liquid is needed, add beef broth.*

Index

Index

Index